COPING WITH EVIL

COPING WITH EVIL

BRUCE H. MCCAUSLAND

Lindisfarne Books
2006

LINDISFARNE BOOKS
www.lindisfarne.org
AN IMPRINT OF ANTHROPOSOPHIC PRESS, INC.
610 Main Street, Suite 1
Great Barrington, MA, 01230

Copyright © 2006 by Lindisfarne Books. All rights reserved. No part of this publication may be reproduced, stored in a retrieval system, or transmitted in any form or by any means, electronic, mechanical, photocopying, recording, or otherwise without the prior written permission of the publisher.

COVER IMAGE: *Licht und Finsternis (Luzifer und Ahriman)* by Rudolf Steiner
COVER AND BOOK DESIGN: William (Jens) Jensen

LIBRARY OF CONGRESS CATALOGING-IN-PUBLICATION DATA

McCausland, Bruce H.
Coping with evil / Bruce H. McCausland.
p. cm.
Includes bibliographical references and index.
ISBN-13: 978-1-58420-044-4 (alk. paper)
ISBN-10: 1-58420-044-8 (alk. paper)
1. Good and evil—Miscellanea. 2. Anthroposophy. I. Title.
BF1999.M4525 2006
170—dc22
2006027427

Contents

	Foreword	ix
1.	The Two Faces of Evil	1
2.	A Closer Look	13
3.	A Holoscopic Look at the Human Being	33
4.	The Eternal Feminine	61
5.	Repentance, the Ultimate Paradigm Shift	77
6.	Restitution and Redemption	99
7.	The Afterimage	117
8.	Mysterium Magnum	127
9.	Thoughtworthy Themes	139
	Epilogue: Redeeming the Apple	151
	Appendices	
	1. Committee for the Scientific Investigation of Claims of the Paranormal	155
	2. The Reappearance of the What???	159
	Notes	165
	Bibliography	171

THIS BOOK IS DEDICATED TO THE SPIRIT OF TRUTH

"I have much more to tell you, but you cannot grasp it now. But when the Spirit of truth comes, He will guide you into the whole truth: for He will not speak on His own authority but will tell what is told Him, and will announce to you the things that are to come."

—JOHN 16:12,13 (Williams translation)

Appreciation

To the early readers of this work—too many to name here—I express my sincere appreciation for their numerous fine suggestions. Three of these individuals I wish to single out for their unique skills in plastic surgery: Jens Jensen, editor at Lindisfarne Press, for deftly removing the warts and other nasty bits; and my friends Martin Croes, and Robert O'Brian, microsurgeons each, who donated several days of their precious time to complete the cosmetic procedure.

Buffalo, New York
Michaelmas, 2006

Foreword

The brutal 9/11 attacks on the two great symbols of American power, the World Trade Center and the Pentagon, were a shocking wake-up call. But wake-up to what? To the typical response of retaliation, vengeance, and further bombings? Perhaps. But even more to the point, they call us to *wake up now* to a deeper comprehension of evil itself. After all, both sides in this terrible battle see the other as evil; one is called the "Axis of Evil," while the other is often referred to as the "Great Satan." Which side is correct? Can they both be right? Could they both be wrong?

Evil is a vast and fascinating challenge which concerns us all, ranging from the hidden, cringing recesses of the human psyche all the way out to the expansive reaches of the mythopoeic cosmos. It has been a subject of concerned study by serious scholars and thinkers in practically every field of human endeavor. Since evil is the cause of so much suffering, the goal has generally been to understand and overcome it. Yet how successful have these scholars been? Indeed, is it possible to understand and subdue evil? As we begin a new millennium, dare we hope to someday be victorious over the dreadful scourge we call evil? Thus far, all efforts seem to have been futile. Evil persists despite our best efforts.

The disputatious realms of morality and ethics, and their manifold schools of advocates, are legitimate concerns for anyone seriously attempting to study evil. Equally disputatious is that field of theology called eschatology, the one concerned with questions of the last days and the "final judgement." But why so much dispute? Philosophers, psychologists, bio-ethicists, and even geneticists have entered the fray, each espousing a favored position and a remedy, or at least an explanation.

Perhaps the most disputatious of all is what philosophers call the "theological problem of evil." (To give an idea of what a hot potato this baby is, I've often heard theologians refer to it as the "*philosophic* problem of evil.") This fascinating enigma has perplexed both camps for many centuries. Simply stated it consists of three premises or assertions: 1) God is almighty, or omnipotent; 2) God is perfectly good; and 3) evil exists. If evil does exist, it would follow logically that a perfectly good God would attempt to eradicate it: yet He appears unable to do so, thus forfeiting his omnipotence. The other horn of the dilemma (technically not a dilemma, but an inconsistent triad or *antilogism*) is equally untenable. It states that evil exists because God does not want to obliterate it. To accept this alternative, however, would be to deny God's goodness. This seemingly irresolvable problem has been one of the major factors contributing to the vast schism that has separated knowledge from faith and science from religion throughout modern times. It is an important wedge, or cleaver, that we cannot ignore. For centuries, philosophers and theologians alike have proposed various *theodicies* (Leibniz' term for suggested answers to this paradox), whereas some have just ignored the problem. Most branches of orthodox Christianity refuse to deny any of the three premises, while the "scientific" thinker, until now, has been unable to accept all three premises because of their mutually contradictory nature. It will be one task of this work to address this "problem of evil" without denying any of its three premises, and to work our way to a theodicy, or suggested solution, worthy of consideration.

Because the chasm between scientific and religious thinkers is so vast and so important in any serious consideration of the question of evil, we will introduce and attempt to resolve two additional "cleavers," or open wounds, that separate them. We call these the *cleaver of incredulity* and the *cleaver of perceived injustices*, both of which we will examine during the course of this work.

Evil permeates our lives—our actions, our will impulses, as well as our life of feeling and thinking. People in business, for example, are called on every day to make decisions that may be considered good or bad—not only as they may affect the success of the business, or bottom line but, more importantly from our perspective, how they affect other people. When Enron, that former corporate giant, was about to implode, and when its top management unloaded their own stock while barring Enron stock sales by its employees, many saw it as an evil act. Scientists, too, may be tempted to "cook" their test results to favor one interpretation of data over another and, as a result, cause unforeseen grief many years later as those false results and misinterpretations are applied to people's lives. At first, all this may be done quite innocently from their perspective just to encourage funding (scientists and executives of the Tobacco Institute come to mind here). In the process, however, the precious commodities of objectivity and truth are tossed onto the scrap heap.

Authorities such as physicians may calamitously affect the entire course of their patients' lives through carelessly spoken phrases. Politicians who appeal to emotions, greed, and fear instead of reason can thoughtlessly incite acts as serious as assassinations, riots, and war. In each of these examples, the intent may not have been to do evil, but the results speak for themselves. The question of evil permeates everything we do, especially when our deeds affect others. Yet clearly, the many approaches over the centuries to resolve this problem have not been successful.

Isn't it clear that a whole new approach is needed? That evil must be addressed at its very roots? Much of what follows may be an easy target for ridicule, which seems to be the fashion today in certain circles—to prove one's superiority through a deft ability to slice apart another's views, often without giving them serious consideration. Slice away! But if you, the reader, are willing to set aside preconceptions and prejudices, if you have the good will to enter this important arena with an open mind and, since we will be dealing with such inimical realities, if you have a fair amount of courage, then these pages will provide an exciting adventure worthy of the effort. We will meet the main antagonists of our drama immediately, in the first chapter, while the protagonists will be introduced in good time.

If this book helps increase awareness of the mighty drama playing itself out on the various stages of human endeavor, then it will have accomplished much of its purpose. For, in my considered opinion, the only evil greater than evil itself is *indifference* to evil.

We will approach this important subject from what I have come to call a "holoscopic" perspective. As we introduce and deepen our acquaintance with this new art, or concept, of holoscopy, we will attempt at the same time to gain an ever deeper insight into the function of evil.

As aspiring holoscopists we will approach our subject in the manner of a scientist studying a disease. Such a study, which hopes to find a cure, should not be confused with advocacy, regardless of how close we get to the contamination. In the process, we will attempt to shed some light on the mystery of evil, that ages-old *mysterium iniquitatus* that has intrigued, tormented, and perplexed people ever since the "fall," when we descended into matter and began our dark journey through this school of hard knocks. The time has come when science of the spirit must be recognized and heeded. Evil, which is the subject of so much unenlightened rancor, disputation, and vituperation on the one hand, and passive indifference on the other, must be dealt with objectively and scientifically before we will ever find a rational resolution to its many challenges. This is the only way that we can be active players instead of passive pawns in this turbid game of life.

Fortunately, science of the spirit exists, and we must turn to this little recognized area of highly disciplined endeavor for the answers to the perplexing problems that confront us today. Holoscopy, the discipline we are attempting to bring forth here, can be seen as an introduction to spiritual science.

We will be drawing from the works of several authors, notably Rudolf Steiner (1861–1925), the Austrian philosopher and spiritual scientist whose observations in a wide variety of fields, including architecture, medicine, agriculture, the arts and pedagogy are just now beginning to attract wider attention in North America; and his contemporary, Sri Aurobindo (1872–1950), the Indian Hindu master whose English upbringing and Cambridge education equipped him to guide western minds into the otherwise labyrinthine wisdom teachings of the East— this despite his rather florid literary style.

It is owed primarily to Rudolf Steiner that we are now able to speak of spiritual science as a legitimate area of study. Scattered throughout his thousands of lectures and scores of written works are numerous indications for a deeper, more penetrating understanding of evil. Our intention will be to sort through them and see if we can come up with a coherent and meaningful interpretation of the subject at hand. A previous acquaintance with Steiner's works should not be necessary. For those who wish to pursue Rudolf Steiner's works in greater depth, the bibliography provides a list of books, most of which are currently available.

Perhaps one of the reasons why Steiner's and Aurobindo's names are not on everyone's lips is because they do not provide easy reading, and I suspect they planned it that way. Neither of them intended to become pop stars. A certain amount of inner work is needed to gain a foothold in the frequently bewildering spiritual realms they describe. By doing this work their concepts are enlivened in our consciousness. Moreover, both men challenge us with an embarrassment of riches. If their achievements were less far-reaching and diverse, people could more easily come to terms with them, and by now both would almost certainly be quite famous. But famous or not, what these modern-day seers had to say about evil is worthy of study. Moreover, by citing two such disparate sources—one a Christian initiate and the other a Hindu guru—we can easily maintain a more balanced perspective as we pursue this fascinating and important subject.

Many volumes have been written about the subject of evil; it has intrigued serious thinkers for millennia. Here, we will attempt to show that the scientific-philosophic mode of thinking—the proper insistence on provability and verification—can now be reconciled with the so-called religious mode, which draws more on the *authority* of ancient texts than on whether they can be proven scientifically. The various cleavers that have been driven between these two equally reputable schools will be examined in the hope that we can dissolve them by means of our good will and serious consideration of the issues involved. This is no easy task, and many of the arguments that follow are presented here more as seed thoughts than as self-evident, complete, defensible positions. Many of these discussions really require a volume each, so it is hoped that you, the reader, will tend these seeds well in the most fertile areas of your consciousness. Who knows? Perhaps some of you may even feel inspired to join this battle royal with evil.

We can only feel admiration for great thinkers such as Blaise Pascal who, more than 350 years ago, saw this huge chasm developing, and wrote in his *Pensées*, "The heart has its reasons, which reason does not know.... It is the heart which experiences God, and not the reason. This, then, is faith: God felt by the heart, not by the reason." He follows this observation with these potent words: "Thought constitutes the greatness of man.... All our dignity consists, then, in thought. By it we must elevate ourselves, and not by space and time which we cannot fill. Let us endeavor, then, to think well; this is the principle of morality." *Think well!* May we ever harken to these great words! Indeed, "think well!" may be seen as the main plea of this work.

Before we begin, however, an additional point should be mentioned. The excursion we are about to take can be bewildering, even frightening, and for me to ask you to embark on it without some assurance that there is a safe destination would be asking too much of your good will and trust. So let me assure you there is a safe haven awaiting us, and it is important to keep this in mind as we traverse these stormy seas. We will even catch glimpses of it during the first leg of our journey, "The Two Faces of Evil."

Coping with Evil

Chapter One

The Two Faces of Evil

If thou canst not love the vilest worm and the foulest of criminals,
how canst thou believe that thou hast accepted God in thy Spirit?
—Sri Aurobindo, *The Hour of God*

Could You Embrace That?
I said to God, "Let me love you."
And He replied, "which part?"
"All of you, all of you," I said.
"Dear," God spoke, "you are as a mouse wanting to impregnate
   a tiger who is not even in heat. It is a feat way
beyond your courage and strength.
You would run from me if I removed my mask."
I said to God again,
"Beloved, I need to love you—every aspect, every pore."
And this time God said,
"There is a hideous blemish on my body, though it is such an
   infinitesimal part of my being—could you kiss that if it
   were revealed?"
"I will try, Lord, I will try."
And then God said, "That blemish is all the hatred and
cruelty in this world."
—St Thomas Aquinas, as quoted in
Love Poems from God: Twelve Sacred Voices from the East and West

None of us wants to be a tool of evil. At least we can hope this is the case. How then does this insidious interloper worm its way into our lives? Clearly, good intentions are not enough. Despite our best intentions, evil still exists in us and in the world. Where, then, does it come from?

Actual, living spiritual beings, working for both good and ill, are behind the perceptible forces that function in our daily lives. This shouldn't be too hard to accept if we realize that, for example, there's a watchmaker behind every watch and there are architects, engineers, and building crews behind every building. The fact that we can't see them operating behind the scenes in no way reduces our knowledge of their existence. Why then should it be difficult to accept the existence of intelligent beings, including the so-called "hindering beings," behind something as beautiful and complex as a human being? They are present; we just can't see them. At least we can't see them with our physical eyes.

Initiates such as Aurobindo and Steiner were able to see such beings. With their heightened clarity of consciousness and with precision and scientific repeatability, they were able to explore the far-reaching depths of the spiritual worlds and then, based on their researches in these realms, they could verify, amplify, and enrich the profound truths handed down to us from the world's great religions and age-old wisdom teachings, including insights into the nature and behavior of powers opposing the forces we call "good."

Individuals such as Steiner and Aurobindo may not be unique, but their spiritual work undertaken before a derisive and superficial world required great courage. This is especially true of Steiner, who worked in a Europe drenched in materialism. The time had come, however, for the breakthrough, making possible a heightened awareness of spiritual worlds. These two preeminent thinkers, while quite different in background, style, and approach, made remarkably similar observations about their spiritual investigations, including those into the subject at hand.

"Bah! What rubbish! Nobody can make such claims." That was my reaction shortly after starting to read my first Steiner book back in the late 1960s. I threw the book down and stormed out of the room, no longer able to sit down. Such was my anger. Later I learned that what shocked me so much in those first few pages was mild compared to some of the things I was to read later in his other books. Fortunately, I was able to overcome my initial antipathy.

If you have a similar reaction as you read these words, take heart. You are not asked to believe anything that Steiner, Aurobindo, or I have to say. You are asked only to test what is written. Test it just as a businessperson might assess a supplier as a standard quality-control procedure or as a scientist must test an instrument's accuracy. Test the thoughts here for internal coherence. Test them against everything you know to be good and beautiful and true. Test them for their practical application in daily life. Test them against the great wisdom teachings of the ages, including the Bible, and see if these works don't emerge from this encounter with a deeper and greater relevance than you may have glimpsed before. If you perform this experiment properly, with an inner effort that brings great teachings alive in the soul, then one day you too may be able to say (to paraphrase Judge Thomas Troward): Certain of these great spiritual insights are true, not just because they're in the Holy Bible, but rather, the Bible is holy and true because these great spiritual insights are in it.[1]

It is in the nature of today's healthy understanding that knowledge should be tested systematically before we accept it as true. We can no longer rely on outside authority to tell us what to believe. In medicine, for example, we often get a second opinion; why not a second, and a third, opinion in matters of the soul and spirit? Then, after hearing and carefully weighing a variety of opinions in these matters, we can begin to formulate our own view. Paradoxically, the less tenaciously we adhere to these various opinions, the more valuable they become. Only by rising step-by-step to perspectives that transcend dogma can we awaken our thinking sufficiently to see truth, beauty and goodness in their own light, and by this light to recognize evil, ugliness, illusion, and deceit for what they are, and to understand their significant roles in our evolution.

When we observe evil from such a perspective, we are led to a startling conclusion. We see not a good/evil continuum, but an evil/evil continuum with good in the center as the *golden mean.* One extreme is as bad as the opposite one. Is simpering cowardice any better than foolhardy bravado? Is a tight-fisted miser better than a spendthrift?

There's a "teaching image" I like to use at this point that will help us illuminate and organize our ideas and impressions. I call it the "great vertical polarity of evil." The lower extreme is characterized by an excessive preoccupation with materialism. Here the forces of gravity and attraction to material goods predominate, which are particularly strong in our time. Their adherents can be found in business and the professions and wherever the desire for possessions and power predominate. It is typical for all those who see technology as the bright, shiny future for humanity, to the exclusion of the spirit. Business, the professions, and technology are not themselves evil; it is the excessive preoccupation with money and power that does such harm. The stunning achievements of science and technology during the past century alone are quite awesome and admirable and deserve our highest respect—the lunar landing, for example. Whether or not we agree with the purpose of the lunar mission, we have to admire the skill and cooperation among the many team members who made it possible to place human footprints on the moon.

Yet, are we misguided when we look to science and technology for answers to the most important questions facing humanity today? Sri Aurobindo seemed to think so. In his provocative collection of aphorisms contained in *The Hour of God and Other Writings* we find: "To see the composition of the Sun or the lines of Mars is doubtless a great achievement; but when thou hast the instrument that can show thee a man's soul as thou seest a picture, then thou wilt smile at the wonders of physical science as the playthings of babies."[2] Strong words from the Pundit of Pondicherry. Such words could easily be passed over with a shrug of self-satisfied superiority, yet thousands of thoughtful seekers have found great wisdom in Aurobindo's words.

Another example of this lower polarity is extreme nationalism and chauvinism, the unshakeable belief that one's own blood line and racial pool is superior to all others, and the consequent hatred toward and prejudice against other races and nations. Indeed, fundamentalism itself, doctrinaire thinking in all its guises, generates evil actions. We will return to the question of fundamentalism later.

Perhaps we can get a better view of this bottom polarity if we contrast it with its opposite, top extreme. Here we find dewy-eyed dreamers, directed in life from "on high" by some mysterious and untested channeled source; we find people who float through life, unable to keep a real job for more than a year or two; we find beautiful, artistic souls who can't manage their personal affairs or keep their feet on the ground. These are the denizens of the upper extreme. They are frequently drawn to light movements and ascending causes such as some aspects of the new age movement which fail to develop adequate roots in the dark and tangled earth. Such souls may be helped by a good dose of daily, routine discipline to balance out their untethered elusive and high-flying exaltations. As Peter Caddy—cofounder of the new-age Findhorn Community in northern Scotland—was fond of saying: "We have too many new-age poets. What we need are new-age plumbers." Perhaps these sensitive souls are trying to escape from the cold, heartless, calculating machinations of the lower extreme by embracing a potentially equally dangerous temptation at the upper.

We now have a sketch of these two great polarities. To add color, and to fulfil the mission of this book, we must now steel ourselves to meet the two powerful spiritual beings who operate behind the scenes of this grand drama: Lucifer and Ahriman. Unfortunately, the Bible (through its many translations and re-writings through the ages by well-meaning though uninitiated scribes) comes down to us with a slightly confounded picture of its main antagonists, the Devil and Satan. It is probably for this reason, and because of the immense amount of emotional baggage attached to these names, that Steiner chose the more emotionally neutral names *Lucifer* and *Ahriman*. We'll try to hold on to that neutrality as we explore their inner nature.

Let's try an experiment. Imagine living in a world without evil. There is nothing wrong in this mythical place; we can do no wrong and have reached a certain level of perfection in our development where we dreamily bask in the effulgent glory of the angels and archangels who minister to us in this wondrous realm. Words fashioned for our present-day earthly world totally fail to describe such conditions. We are perfectly content. Nothing can harm us. We have no cares or worries because all our needs are met so perfectly that we aren't even aware of having such needs. Divine bliss! Infinite provender! Without so much as a rock to turn or a field to till from one sleepy day to the next. It is the primal womb of innocence.

Listen to Milton's luscious words:

> Thus was this place
> A happy rural seat of various view;
> Groves whose rich trees wept odorous gums and balm,
> Others whose fruit burnished with golden rind,
> Hung amiable, Hesperian fables true,
> If true, here only, and of delicious taste.
> Betwixt them lawns, or level downs, and flocks
> Grazing the tender herb, were interposed;
> Or palmy hillock, or the flowery lap
> of some irriguous valley spread her store,
> Flowers of all hue, and without thorn the rose.
> Another side, umbrageous grots and caves
> Of cool recess, o'er which the mantling vine
> Lays forth her purple grape, and gently creeps
> Luxuriant.[3]

Milton, of course, had to use physical images to convey what he saw so clearly with his heart's eye. And perhaps his physical blindness was even an asset in this task, deepening his sensitivity to the soul power of the English language in building up such evocative images.

Returning to our exercise and our look at paradise, one fateful day (actually days and nights don't exist in this mythic realm, but significant time has passed) we are approached by a being of immense beauty who evokes in us a powerful symphony of very new feelings. "See these gods (the angelic hierarchy) in their majestic glory? You, too, can be like them," he tells us. A curious new sensation begins to stir inwardly. "But despite all their glory," he continues, "you can have something even they don't have. They don't have freedom, but *I* can make you free. You will have the ability to forge your own destiny. Truly, you shall be as gods!" Well, how could anyone turn down an offer like that? "I have the power to give you just a small taste of this freedom. And once you taste it, you'll know what I mean. Here, take just one little bite and see."

We have just met Lucifer, the first of our friendly enemies. Now we see, all right, but we see with physical rather than spiritual eyes. Thanks to this great temptation and our response to it (which we cannot be held wholly accountable for, because we were not fully conscious at the time), we now live in a *physical* world and not in the divine spiritual world. According to spiritual investigation, in paradise, before the "fall," we were much more ethereal than we are today, and much more susceptible to the influence of divine and other spiritual beings. But our consciousness in that proto-human condition was dim and dreamy. It became necessary for us to experience dense physical matter so that we could develop the power to think and to reason and so that our "I," or Ego, could begin to develop. This physical world gives us a firm center within our own being.[4]

Sri Aurobindo describes the same event from a different perspective:

> *Ignorance* means Avidya, the separative consciousness and the egoistic mind and life that flow from it and all that is natural to the separative consciousness and the egoistic mind and life. The Ignorance is the result of a movement by which the cosmic Intelligence separated itself from the light of the supermind (the divine Gnosis) and lost the Truth—truth of being, truth of divine consciousness, truth of force and action, truth of Ananda. As a

result, instead of a world of integral truth and divine harmony created in the light of the divine Gnosis, we have a world founded on the past truths of an inferior cosmic Intelligence in which all is half-truth, half-error.[5]

Through the looking-glass of this quotation, we may very well be getting a peek at Lucifer's cosmic past and his role in setting the scene for the fall. But Lucifer's functions in the microcosm, that is, *in us*, are no less significant. As a tempter he is tenacious, goading us into believing that we are peerless, and that our accomplishments (unfortunately so little understood), are vastly superior to their actual worth. He flatters us inwardly through our own subtle centers of self-love. Yet, as Steiner cautions, Lucifer is needed for our proper development. It is precisely the luciferic influence in us that permeates the arts, for example, inspiring artists to rise above mere naturalism and mediocrity. He works in our supraconscious, inspiring us to ever higher levels of artistic achievement. At the same time, luciferic activity leads to a human tendency to see the world from the airy perspective of a bird. All those wonderful attempts to inspire a return to the Golden Age by loosening our connection with physical reality, to soar above the actual circumstance, point to Lucifer. This is also true of the impulse that tends to diminish our interest in other human beings.[6]

We can see how Lucifer has both a positive and negative side—or, better, how we can either benefit from him or succumb to his inimical powers, depending on how we respond to his influence. This is a fascinating point and one that bears a closer look. Consider fire, for example. When out of control, it can be one of the most destructive forces in nature, yet in its proper place (at least from our perspective), fire is used every day to warm our houses and cook our food. In a similar way Lucifer, unchecked in the soul, can produce overwhelming passions, monstrous obsessions, and destructive ego inflations. And yet, a little luciferic enthusiasm may help a student (for example) leaven the otherwise dull loaf of an intellectually collapsed and deadened ahrimanic curriculum.

Lucifer has his uses, and a holoscopic approach can help us recognize, appreciate, and implement them. The holoscopist is free to choose; to soar awhile with Lucifer, thus gaining higher and wider perspectives on the phenomena at hand and at their interrelatedness with other phenomena, diverse views of their causes (note the plural), and their immediate and long-range effects.

Holoscopy may be seen as a prelude to spiritual science— "Spiritual Science 101." In spiritual science, however, the "101" course does not last a mere semester but for many years. It calls for not only accepting, but also for looking at the positive aspects of what may initially seem to be the most negative of situations. It requires more than just looking at the figure *or* the ground, but at the figure *and* the ground. When observing two people disputing some point, the holoscopist attempts to embrace, as warmly as possible, both sides of the argument. This is not to say that holoscopists don't have their own opinions—they do, but their views are formed after carefully deliberating both sides of an issue; they are not simply knee-jerk responses to one side or the other. As Aurobindo puts it: "When O eager disputant, thou hast prevailed in a debate, then art thou greatly to be pitied, for thou hast lost a chance of widening knowledge."[7]

Aurobindo's dictum applies equally to watching a debate. Let's say A and B are having a hot debate about an important topic. When A speaks, the holoscopist attempts to enter A's arguments with as much inner warmth, sympathy, and understanding as possible, even if the holoscopist disagrees with the speaker. The same applies to B's argument. This is a truly rewarding exercise and helps immensely in transcending biases to gain a higher perspective. Televised debates provide many opportunities to practice this exercise.

Now let's see if we can embrace both the positive and negative sides of Lucifer and Ahriman and the vast spectrum between them. Even the effort is worthwhile, for in the effort is the growth. "No pain, no gain" is more than just a clever slogan.

If Lucifer is the lord of illusion, Ahriman can be called the lord of deceit and lies. While Lucifer shines in our *supra*conscious mind, Ahriman lurks in the dark recesses of our *sub*conscious mind. He is the one who prompts us to tell those little not-so-white lies, like "The check's in the mail," or "I'm working on it; it's almost finished," for a job not yet begun. Ahriman is the "prince of darkness" of Zoroastrian writings; his archenemy was Ahura Mazda, the great wise lord of the Sun (later called "Ohrmuzd"). Ahura Mazda should not be confused with Lucifer. The two are as different from each other, one could say, as the Sun is from Venus. True, the name *Lucifer* means "light bearer," but the confusion over the name becomes clear in the light of the ancient occult saying *"Christus verus Luciferus"* (Christ is the true light-bearer).

As we pore through Rudolf Steiner's lectures and writings and the Bible, as well as other sources, in trying to understand Ahriman (and Lucifer, too, for that matter), we might reach a point where we think we comprehend him. Then, out of the blue, an attribute arises that seems wholly inconsistent with what we have learned. Lucifer, for example, as a vile serpent from one perspective, and as a beautiful, radiant being from another. Yet with further reflection, we are soon able to incorporate each new insight and image into our view and thus enhance our understanding. Lucifer and Ahriman are living spiritual beings, with long histories and existential complexities. Would any of *us* feel well served if someone tried to describe us completely in a scant paragraph or two? Even in this book-length study of evil, we can only hope to lay the foundations for a deeper understanding of Lucifer and Ahriman.

Steiner describes Lucifer as a proud spirit who likes to soar into the heights where lofty visions open out. He describes Ahriman as a morally lonely spirit, unwilling to make his presence known. He works more in our unconscious or subconscious, where he conjures his materialistic judgments. Steiner cites a reasonably accurate portrayal of our proper relationship to Ahriman: "Be calm and alert. Your opponent the devil is always prowling about like a roaring lion, trying to devour you" (I Peter 5:8). Ahriman really does prowl in the hidden parts of human nature, our subconscious. He strives to reach his earthly goal by diverting human subconscious forces to himself in order to attain different spiritual ends than those in the proper stream of human evolution.[8]

And further, regarding Ahriman's earthly goals, the spiritual researcher tells us that everything connected with the lust to rule over fellow humans, all that is opposed to healthy social impulses, is ahrimanic. So we have Lucifer and those who lose interest in their fellow human beings on the one hand; and we have those who want to take advantage of all human failings to gain control over as many people as possible on the other; these people are under the influence of Ahriman.[9]

A popular expression, "The devil made me do it," can be seen even on tee-shirts. It sounds a doubly insidious note, because this attempt to be cute not only encourages dubious behavior, but it also contradicts a main theme of this book: The devil cannot make us do anything. Lucifer and Ahriman exist so that we can garner enough strength to resist their efforts to incite evil. The best way we can do this is to get to know them and to see how they operate. We will examine their various *modi operandi* in the following chapters.

To end this chapter on a positive note, I'd like to offer a perspective of evil that was presented by a being named Hilarion, as channeled through a friend who lives just outside of Toronto and who writes under the name Maurice B. Cooke. First, however, we should note that there are those who caution us about following channeled advice, and to that I would add a second caution. Not only may the source of the channeled material be uncertain, but the channel may also be placed in a vulnerable position. Nevertheless, the merit of this very helpful analogy is obvious:

> The dark ones ... act as testing agents for the race of man, as forces whose task it is to weed out from among the human flock the souls whose dedication, wisdom, and insight are not developed enough to allow them to move forward into the higher ground of spiritual achievement. This can be compared to the effect of the wolf on a herd of caribou. Among the caribou are the old, the sick, the congenitally weak specimens. The wolf attacks only these defective caribou, and would never think of wasting its energy

trying to chase or bring down healthy specimens. By weeding out the weaker ones, the wolf ensures that the herd remains strong.[10]

Chapter Two

A Closer Look

> "If you perceive a man as good, think of emulating him;
> If you perceive a man as bad, think of examining your own heart."
>
> —Confucius, *Analects*

Let's try another imaginative exercise. With your mind's eye, picture living as a young child in a small European town during the late Middle Ages. One misty autumn afternoon, the itinerant storyteller arrives. What excitement you feel in anticipation of the campfire, as all the townspeople begin to assemble in the hazy early evening to hear his wondrous tales.

In the gathering gloom he begins to spin his yarn. Perhaps this night's adventure is of King Arthur and his round table, Percival, Gawain, and the rest; or the mythic tale of how Loki slew Baldur with the aid of the mystical, unearthly forces of mistletoe. Whatever the yarn, whether myth, saga, or legend, with your eyes closed and with intense inner participation and awe, you weave it into fine, colorful soul-warming fabric. Some adults of this rustic village have similar living reverberations within their souls, because they have opened themselves and made themselves vulnerable to the mighty imaginations of the scenes portrayed by the skilled, insightful master storyteller. Later, and for many nights thereafter during the coming winter months, you relive in your dreams the great adventures you yourself had experienced by dint of your active, inner sense of awe-filled wonder, because you had listened so attentively, so actively, to the magical tales of the storyteller.

Now we move ahead a few centuries and closer to our time. *Radio* is the new storyteller and the audience is no longer visible to the storyteller, just as the storyteller is invisible to the audience. Nor are they gathered around a campfire but, quite likely, huddled behind a steering wheel in a cold, metallic, and plastic isolation box on wheels. The all-important interpersonal human contact has disappeared.

Then, in the late 1940s, along came an even greater wonder: *television*. Like radio, it soon quit rerunning the classics, whether those of music, poetry, or drama, but it still tried to be a positive influence in those early days. Back in the mid-1950s, I recall playing the title role on a local television station in the medieval morality play *Everyman* for a university drama class. On another station that same year I performed in Aeschylus's *Prometheus Bound;* heady stuff for local commercial television. Soon, we were promised even better viewing (certainly better talent) as, one by one, the local network affiliates were connected by cable to others across the country. Great concerts from Carnegie Hall, live! But in our naïveté, we didn't see the greedy few and the vast fortunes they could make by taking control of our precious television and appealing not to the highest, most noble and pure qualities in the audience, but to the lusts and passions of our lowest instincts.

Today we still have wonderful vestiges of culture on our television, but mostly we have talk shows with people screaming at one another and rudely interrupting whoever is speaking in an incessant demand to make their points heard; we have televangelists passionately gesticulating and imploring that our souls cannot be saved but will suffer eternal damnation unless we interpret the Bible exactly as they do (and send them a few hundred dollars so they can continue preaching "the word of God"); and we have the endless parade of sex, violence, seductive commercials and bawdy comedians on the rapidly increasing number of channels. Among the most popular programs are wrestling shows with violence and sexual overtones, and professional sports, the more violent the better. This is what passes for heroism today! According to recent news reports, one out of five NFL football players are typically under indictment or are being investigated for possible involvement in serious crimes of violence. Gone are the bucolic days when noble kings and knights and virtuous maidens captivated our imaginations. In their place are brutish football heroes, drug-crazed rock stars, and sleazy talk-show hosts. Why this descent into violence, vulgarity, greed, and lust? Who or what is behind it all?

Say hello to Ahriman. Do you think human beings invented television, the computer, and biotechnology all on their own? In fact they had a great deal of assistance from hidden, spiritual realms. Ahriman placed them, oh so skillfully, into our eager hands. He has the power to whisper his secrets of an earthly paradise into the awaiting ears of inventors and scientists all over the world, especially in the West. Quite literally, he speaks from the deep recesses of our unconscious wherever he finds willing ears. He is infinitely cleverer than any human, and he uses his cleverness to convince us that our future, our salvation, lies here on Earth. "Forget the spirit" is his message or, at best, whatever we call the spirit, which he wants us to see as nothing more than an invisible, worthless excrescence of matter. He knew that, if television started out with the trash we see today, a large segment of his potential audience would be so shocked they'd never buy into it. As impatient as Ahriman is, he had to play his cards slowly and carefully and gradually lead us into trusting him as an honest dealer, so he could prepare us for his big bluff. To him we're just sucker bait, and most of us don't even know that we're sitting at his card table as we clutter our lives with his many enticing contraptions.

Who cares about all that, some might ask; we now have *virtual* reality. We can soar through cyberspace and go anywhere we want. What wonderful gifts your friend Ahriman is giving us! Look at all the people we can contact on the Internet. We can be in touch with the whole world with just the press of a few buttons on the keyboard and the click of a mouse. Well, it seems obvious that the only thing we're really in touch with is the keyboard, and a lifeless, electronic rodent on the end of a limp, grey wire. Those and a few million blinking pixels on a cold, glass screen. Yet Ahriman's gifts, if rightly used, are wonderful. The question is, are we strong enough to use them in the right way? Ahriman wishes to control us; he wants human beings to be extensions of his machines, not the other way around. He wants to steal our capacity to think; he wants to steal our very souls and control us. Ahriman offers us great gifts with his one hand, while he picks our pockets with the other. In place of the heartwarming pictures we wove in our imaginations out of the raw stuff of the storyteller during the Middle Ages, we have staging, lighting, casting, props, and everything else pre-ordained for us on the flickering screen in our living rooms, offices, kitchens, and even bedrooms. He's robbing us of our imaginations, too, and everything else that makes us truly human.

Some believe that little children can learn the intricacies of mathematics with the aid of calculators. But calculators just rob children of their inner capacity to do math—all those hapless children taught to rely on the calculator for their answers are actually just learning which keys to push on a calculator; they're not really learning mathematics but external shortcuts to the answers. The introduction of computers into our primary grades is even more insidious. Many educators think of computers and interactive television as "learning machines" that teach our children valuable lessons. Instead, however, they rob young people of their teachers and the real lessons of warm human contact, cooperation, and creative artistic expression. We are becoming a nation of sleepwalkers by refusing to see this "open secret"—open, that is, to anyone who has the courage to face reality.[1]

Ahriman wants to control us, and he is succeeding. Everything that pits one faction against another, whether through racism, nationalism, religious bigotry, are all his impulses and tools for dividing and conquering human beings. At the same time, everything that impels us toward uniformity—cataloging human beings as mere numbers, applying statistics to social behavior, and controlling people through the latest, most sophisticated advertising techniques—is ahrimanic *and* luciferic. The two often work together. And what will come of all this? What will be the great cultural legacy we leave to our grandchildren? How will we be remembered fifty or a hundred years from now as we begin this new century? Will we leave them a cold, grey, colorless, and impersonal world of subhuman automata, each plugged into a lifeless machine? Or worse, will it be a lifeless world, destroyed by the terrorist acts of the great "war of all against all," a war we are bound to enter into soon if we continue our exclusively materialistic ways Those who have the courage to see what's happening in the real world recognize that the battleground is being prepared today both in us, and around us.

Or perhaps we will be remembered as the ones who had the courage to meet Ahriman face-to-face, even with enthusiasm, while accepting from him those wonderful gifts we can use to benefit humanity while refusing to succumb to his inimical anti-personal, anti-spiritual wiles. The decision is ours. It is a decision we must make now, because Ahriman is approaching the Earth with great speed. The time for his earthly sojourn is at hand. Never mind *Star Wars, Space Raiders,* and other popular fictional dramas; we are faced today with the most exciting adventure in the entire history of the human race. And it is real. It has all the dramatic elements of the greatest story ever told. It is, in fact, the further development of that great story.

Five thousand years ago, Lucifer incarnated in the East, in China. There are no conventional historical records of this momentous event, but his influence permeated for millennia, not only the East but, indeed, the whole world, even to this day. Spiritual science (or in this context, let's call it "initiation science") can tell us of such events, because every thought, feeling or act of will that has ever taken place on Earth is indelibly inscribed in what is called the "akashic record." Initiates of a certain level of attainment can read these records—I won't say with ease, but with accuracy and reliability. At the time of Lucifer's incarnation, there arose in opposition to him certain initiates of the ancient mystery schools of the East. Because of their special training and preparation, those great leaders of humanity were able to thwart Lucifer's intention of drawing us away from Earth and into misty realms of illusion, or pseudo reality. At the same time, with steely resolve and cold, hard unshakable determination, they took from Lucifer such of his many proffered gifts as would be useful and beneficent to the proper course of human development. As a result, today we have the *wisdom* of the East. This was not a "philosophy" of the East, which entails human thinking; that had to wait for Aristotle's time. Rather, it was a great, luciferically inspired wisdom and an abundance of beautiful artistic impulses in architecture, sculpture, painting, dance, and the crafts. Echoes of this ancient wisdom are still reflected in the teachings and observations of great sages such as Confucius and Lao-tzu.

Five thousand years later, coming from the opposite direction, we are faced with the impending incarnation (or incorporation) of Ahriman. Now, however, instead of meeting him with a cold, determined resolve—forces that singe and corrode Lucifer's fiery brilliance—we must meet Ahriman with *enthusiasm*, with warmth of heart for the freedom and dignity of our fellow human beings, and with a firm, unshakable knowledge of the reality of the spiritual worlds. These are the mighty weapons in our arsenal. These forces are inimical and fatal to Ahriman's frigid, heartless, calculating plans for world domination.

Rudolf Steiner sets the stage for us to better understand this unique challenge of our time. He tells us that Ahriman will incorporate in the West in the near future. Ahriman prepares for his coming incarnation by guiding certain forces in evolution so that they will be to his greatest advantage. If we continue in our usual sleepwalk of drowsy unawareness, unwilling or unable to see and recognize certain phenomena in life as the result of Ahriman's preparation for his arrival, evil will come about. The time is at hand when we must learn to recognize the tendencies and events around us that are machinations of Ahriman, preparing the way for his impending incarnation.[2]

Steiner does not say that Ahriman himself is evil, but that evil will result if people continue to live in a state of drowsy unawareness. Even Ahriman has his proper place in the divinely ordained order of the cosmos, just as the wolf has in relation to the caribou herd; otherwise, he would not have been allowed to exist. But we, like the caribou, must become aware of the wolf's whereabouts, or in this case Ahriman's; we must recognize what he's up to and in what kind of terrain he is likely to be stalking us. Like the caribou, we must remain ever-vigilant. Are we up to this task?

Rudolf Steiner presented a wealth of important information about Lucifer and Ahriman (*Ibid*, p. 53 ff.), which I will attempt to summarize. He begins by reminding us that Lucifer incarnated in Asia three thousand years before Christ, and that the original pagan wisdom proceeded from him. We are admonished to give this deep and serious study, because only by understanding the role of Lucifer can we hope to understand Ahriman. If we let our mind's eye survey the vast cultural legacy of the East, and especially the wisdom that some call "pagan" because it precedes Christianity, we can only be in awe of its majesty. It is interesting to see how people sometimes criticize this wisdom of the East because it is not Christian, but how could it be? After all, it is *pre*-Christian. To condemn this vast legacy as being non-Christian is like railing against the Moon at night because it is not the Sun of day. Such criticism is motivated by fear, but those who have a deep understanding of the central role of Christ in earthly evolution have no such fear. For them, the wisdom of the East is a vast reservoir of immensely satisfying, fruitful, and meaningful contemplation. Further, they see much of this wisdom—for example, the Adonis Mysteries and the Isis and Osiris legend of ancient Egypt—as precursors of the advent of Christ and designed to prepare us for that wondrous event, the central mystery of human and earthly evolution.

We would have remained as children if certain initiates of that time had not assumed the mission of applying the luciferic wisdom to the appropriate course of human evolution. It's all the same wisdom. But if it had remained in Lucifer's hands it would have been used improperly. By wresting it from Lucifer and applying it to the furtherance of earthly evolution, however, it became appropriate for the proper advancement of earthly and human evolution. Steiner tells us

> In ancient times the wisdom needed for the progress of humanity could be obtained only from a luciferic source; hence the initiates had to receive it from that source and, at the same time, assume

the obligation to resist the aspirations of the luciferic beings. Lucifer's intention was to convey wisdom to humanity in such a way that it would induce human beings to abandon the path of earthly evolution and take a path leading to a supra-earthly sphere, a sphere aloof from the Earth.... Lucifer wants to abandon the Earth to its fate and to win humankind for a kingdom alien to that of Christ. (*Ibid.*)

Such a purely luciferic kingdom is beautifully and enticingly portrayed in Arthur C. Clarke's fantasy classic *Childhood's End*, in which a number of children undergo a mysterious metamorphosis—one could call it an abnormal "initiation" process—that gives them superhuman, godlike powers. Then, instead of staying with their loved ones on Earth, staying with their parents and friends who made it all possible, and working for their salvation, which would have been the Christian path, they say goodbye to the rest of humanity, leave the Earth, and soar off to an indefinable realm of bliss and cosmic happiness, the path of Lucifer.

On the other hand, if we were to ask what benefits Lucifer had to offer us (What did Lucifer give to human beings in ancient, prehistoric times? What are some of his redeeming qualities?), we would be told that he gave us the rudiments of what later became our capacity to speak and think. Thus, if we really want to turn away and flee from Lucifer (as some strongly advocate), we would also have to cease speaking and thinking in the future. Things are far more complicated than they appear, and this is precisely why an all-encompassing holoscopic perspective is needed to help us progress in our spiritual scientific study of this enormously complex and important question of evil. Simplistic, black-and-white views of right and wrong will no longer suffice.

This naturally leads us to the question of dogmatism. Members of both camps—scientific and religious—are equally guilty of intellectual infractions in this regard. Dogmatism is an attachment to, or greed for, one's own ideas. Like all forms of greed, it leads to a myopic, short-sighted worldview. According to Rudolf Steiner,

These things are part of the initiation science that must gradually come to be known by humanity, although people shrink from such truths because of the kind of education that has been current for centuries in the civilized world. The caricatured figure of Lucifer and Ahriman—the medieval devil—is constantly before their minds, and they have been allowed to grow up in this philistine atmosphere for so long that even today people shudder at the thought of approaching the treasures of wisdom that are intimately and deeply connected with evolution. It is much more pleasant to say, "If I protect myself from the devil, if I give myself to Christ with the simple-heartedness of a child, I will be blessed, and my soul will find salvation." But in its deep foundations, human life is by no means such a simple matter, and it is essential for the future of human evolution that the things we are discussing shall not be withheld from humankind. It must be known that the art of speaking and the art of thinking have become part of evolution only because they were received through Lucifer's mediation.

The luciferic element can still be observed in thinking. Speech, which has for long ages been differentiated and adapted to earthly needs, has already been assailed by Ahriman. He has brought about differentiation, has degraded the one cosmic speech into the various tongues on Earth. Whereas the luciferic tendency is always toward unification, the fundamental tendency of the ahrimanic principle is differentiation.... The moment you generalize or unify you are approaching luciferic thinking. (*Ibid.*)

But a terrible situation would arise if we failed to put orderly and sound thinking in the place of these luciferic generalizations.

That would bring nothing but evil. For then people would grow together with the Earth—that is, with the particular territory on Earth where they are born—and their cultural life would become completely specialized and differentiated.... But the tendency to split up into smaller and smaller groups has been all too apparent because of the catastrophic World War [I]. Chauvinism is increasingly gaining the upper hand, and it will eventually lead people to split up to such an extent that, in the end, a group will consist of a single human being. Things may come to the point where individuals would again split into right and left, and be at war within themselves; left would do battle with right. Such tendencies are even now evident in human evolution. To combat this, a counterweight must be created; and this counterweight can be created only if, like the old wisdom inherent in paganism, a new wisdom, acquired by the free resolve and will of human beings, is infused into earthly culture. This new wisdom must be initiation wisdom. (*Ibid.*)

Next, we encounter one of the most graphic and thought-worthy descriptions of Ahriman to be found in all of Steiner's works. He tells us that, unless we make a conscious effort to acquire this new wisdom, spiritual wisdom, all culture will become ahrimanic, permeating all earthly civilizations. What would happen if we were to follow the strong inclination we have today to let things drift on as they are, without understanding and guiding into right channels those streams which lead to an ahrimanic culture? As soon as Ahriman incarnates at the destined time in the West, the whole of culture would be impregnated with his forces. In addition, through certain stupendous arts he would bring to humanity all the clairvoyant knowledge that, until then, could be acquired only by dint of intense personal effort. We would live on as materialists, eating and drinking as usual, and there would seem to be no need for spiritual efforts. The ahrimanic, materialistic streams would continue their course unimpeded. When Ahriman incorporates in the West at his appointed time, he would establish a great occult school for the practice of magic arts of the greatest grandeur, and what can otherwise be acquired only by strenuous effort would be poured freely over humankind as a gift.

Ahriman will not appear as a kind of hoaxer, playing mischievous tricks on the unsuspecting—no indeed. Lovers of ease who refuse to have anything to do with spiritual science would fall prey to his magic. Through those stupendous magic arts, he would be able to make great numbers of human beings into seers—in such a way, however, that the clairvoyance of one individual would be strictly differentiated from that of another. What one person would see clairvoyantly, a second and a third would not see. Mass confusion would prevail, and in spite of becoming receptive to clairvoyant wisdom, people would inevitably fall into strife over the sheer diversity of their visions. Ultimately, however, we would all be satisfied with our own unique visions, for each would have a unique vision of the spiritual world. All culture on the Earth would then fall prey to Ahriman. We would succumb to Ahriman simply because we would not have acquired by our own efforts what Ahriman is ready and more than willing to give us. The most evil advice would be "Stay just as you are. Ahriman will make all of you clairvoyant if you so desire." And we will desire it, because Ahriman's power will be very great. But the result would be the establishment of Ahriman's kingdom on Earth and the overthrow of everything achieved hitherto through human effort and culture. All the hidden, disastrous tendencies unconsciously cherished by modern human beings would take effect.

Steiner's concern, and the main reason for this work, is that the wisdom of the future—clairvoyant wisdom—must be rescued from the clutches of Ahriman. As mentioned earlier, there is only one kind of wisdom, not two. The issue is whether such wisdom is in the hands of Ahriman or Christ. It cannot come into the hands of Christ unless people fight for it. And they can fight for it only by assimilating the content of spiritual science through their own efforts before the time of Ahriman's appearance on Earth.

It may be confusing to some to say that wisdom does not come into the hands of Christ unless people fight for it. This refers to the risen Christ dwelling in our hearts and souls. Paul spoke of this frequently: "I travail in birth again until Christ be formed in you" (Galatians 4:19). Paul is making a most solemn promise to reincarnate again until we learn this great lesson and waken the dormant Christ within us, when Christ will be formed in us.[3]

Thus we have the great task of spiritual science: to prevent knowledge from becoming, or remaining, ahrimanic. This is by far the most important task facing humanity today. Ahriman's great enemy, insofar as human beings are concerned, is an unshakable, verifiable knowledge of the reality of the spiritual worlds. So even in the various denominational churches it is important that knowledge no longer be withheld. If we were to cling to a simple faith we would condemn our souls to stagnation, and then the wisdom that must be rescued from Ahriman could not find entry. "The point is not whether people do or do not simply receive the wisdom of the future, but whether they work upon it; and those who do must take upon themselves the solemn duty of saving earthly culture for Christ, just as the ancient rishis and initiates pledged themselves not to yield to Lucifer's proviso that humankind be enticed away from the Earth."[4]

But this entails a great struggle, a struggle similar to that waged against Lucifer by the ancient initiates. "Just as it devolved upon the Initiates of the primeval wisdom to wrest from Lucifer that which has become human reason, human intellect, so the insight which is to develop in the future into the inner realities of things must be wrested from the ahrimanic powers. Such are the issues—and these issues play strongly into life itself" (Ibid.).

It should be noted here that spiritual scientific investigation, like any form of scientific work, should be rechecked constantly for accuracy. A very incisive event, an adequate discussion of which is beyond the scope of this work, occurred in Steiner's life during the week between Christmas and New Year's Day at the beginning of 1924, which added greatly to his perceptual powers. Because of that refinement of his clairvoyant faculties, in lectures on August 3 and 4, 1924, he emended his many previous observations about Ahriman's imminent incursion onto the Earth from an "incarnation" to an "incorporation."[5] The difference is technical and need not concern us here, except that the net effect of Ahriman's incorporation may be even stronger than a simple incarnation, because it can occur simultaneously in many people. To quote Steiner on this important point:

Spirits like Ahriman do not exist to incarnate in physical bodies on the Earth. Nevertheless, they can work on the Earth, not by actually incarnating but by incorporating themselves for certain periods of time, when in one or another person there occurs what I mentioned before—a dimming or diversion of consciousness. At such moments, the person provides a vehicle, and Ahriman is able not to actually incarnate but to incorporate himself and work through that human being with that person's faculties.[6] Ahriman can play his game with the soul and spirit as it lives within the body. Above all, when the soul-spiritual is highly gifted and is yet firmly fastened in the body, it can be especially exposed to Ahriman. Ahriman finds his prey in the most gifted people in order to tear [away] that intelligence and remove it far from [the Archangel] Michael. At this point something happens that plays a far greater part in our time than is generally thought. The ahrimanic spirits, although they cannot incarnate, can incorporate themselves; they can temporarily penetrate human souls and permeate human bodies. In such moments, the brilliant and overpowering spirit of ahrimanic intelligence is stronger than anything that an individual possesses—far, far stronger. No matter how intelligent such people may be and how much they may have learned, especially if their physical bodies are thoroughly taken hold of by all their learning, an ahrimanic spirit can incorporate itself in them for a time. Then it is Ahriman who looks out of their eyes, Ahriman who moves their fingers, Ahriman who blows their noses, and Ahriman who walks.[7]

Ahriman's incorporation, according to Steiner, is scheduled for sometime after the turn of the twenty-first century, but he is always in a rush.[8] His appearance at the beginning of the twenty-first century, two thousand years after Christ, is a karmic result of Lucifer's appearance three thousand years before that central, pivotal point in earthly evolution, the Mystery of Golgotha. We cannot avert it, but we must be awake to his influences.

The mythic image of Michael (sometimes depicted as St. George) treading the dragon underfoot pictures real events in our spiritual evolution. The suffix "el," by the way, especially in this case, signifies a divine spiritual being, and Steiner always pronounced *Michael* as three syllables: "Mich-a-el." He has much to say about this prince-regent of all archangels who, since the advent of Christ, commands the battle against Ahriman on various fronts. According to Steiner, Michael in 1879 succeeded in casting the dark, ahrimanic beings out of heaven.[9] Since that time these fallen angels have had to dwell here, in the astral and etheric regions closest to the Earth. Their presence in our environment helps account for the remarkable staying power of an intellectually bankrupt materialism. As we shall see, compelling arguments against a purely matter-bound world-view can now be mounted. Later in this work we will cite a wide array of phenomena which materialists refuse to look at, simply because to do so would shake the foundations of their precious *Weltanschauung*.

Materialism must run its course. It is part of our destiny, the destiny of our present epoch, that materialism seem to prevail for the next four or five hundred years.[10] Materialism prospers best when people think they are not materialists. But the evidence against a purely materialistic world-view is mounting. As we show later in this work, materialists remain so only because they refuse to look with unbiased eyes at anything that challenges their nihilistic, reductionist way of thinking. Why must materialism run its course? Because its presence necessitates that we put something in its place. Just as junk-food fills our belly but fails to nourish us, materialism fills our souls without nourishing them. It creates a void in our soul life which yearns for the truth behind the scenes of external reality. It creates a need for knowledge of spiritual realities. The great task during our present epoch is to study the ways of the Archangel Michael, to find the Michael-forces within our own being, and conquer the evil forces of materialism. "What people in our epoch must learn is the need to wage a fully conscious fight against the evil that is making its way into human evolution" (Ibid.).

In his study of the Apocalypse, Alfred Heidenreich, founding priest of the church of the Christian Community in the English-speaking world, says of Michael:

> And the great conqueror is the Archangel Michael.... It is worthwhile remembering what that name means. It is a challenge. The names of the other archangels mean statements: Raphael, "God Healer"; Gabriel, "God Strength"; but Michael, "Who like God?" It is a challenging question. The old legends say it was the challenge he shouted across the world when Lucifer tried to usurp the throne of God. "Who like God?" was his battle cry.[11]

Since the two work together so often, it is easy to mix Lucifer and Ahriman, one with the other. Even Goethe, to a certain extent, confused the two in the portrayal of Mephistopheles in his great drama *Faust*. Today, however, we no longer have the luxury of glossing over such things through faulty perceptions and simplistic interpretations of the Bible and other great spiritual writings.

According to Steiner, Michael is a stern, taciturn figure of immense power who is humanity's "Sun-Leader" in the battle against evil. In preparation for the modern phase of our battle, Michael bestowed on us a great gift, releasing into our hands from heavenly realms the Cosmic Intelligence that he had administered for long ages on our behalf. It is this Michaelic potential in each of us that Ahriman is trying to seize and control for his own anti-human purposes. He does this by mesmerizing us, dazzling us, with evermore wondrous gifts from his workshop of electro-magnetic-mechanical delights.

Cosmic intelligence is strengthened whenever people work together in groups for its attainment. Such group work helps the individuals involved unfold their Michaelic potential while maintaining balance and perspective. Anthroposophic study group members usually read aloud and discuss spiritual scientific works by Steiner and other spiritual investigators.

Interestingly, Steiner spoke of the pain he felt whenever he saw his words in print, and he even characterized the letters making up words and sentences as "ahrimanic squiggles!" Although he was a hugely prolific writer and lecturer, Steiner was well aware of the fact that his words had to be brought back to life in the hearts and minds of his readers by means of unflagging inner work. Handwriting, however, is not completely ahrimanic. In addition, the spiritual investigator tells us that Ahriman's influence in the art of printing during the modern age has assumed an even deeper significance. Something has now become possible, something that is as great in a brilliant, dazzling way as it is necessary to receive it with a balanced perspective. We must learn to treat such information according to its true significance: Ahriman himself has now appeared *as an author.* Ahriman is a mighty, super-calculating spirit. Although he is not by his very nature fitted to promote the proper evolution of humankind on the Earth in accordance with the intentions of the benevolent gods, he does oppose it. Nevertheless, we must remember that in his own sphere he is not only a thoroughly useful but a beneficent power. Beings, who on one level of world events are benefactors, can be exceedingly harmful on another level. We cannot assume, therefore, that in characterizing works as coming from Ahriman that they must come in for unqualified rebuke. Provided one is conscious of what they are and where they come from, one can even admire them. But their ahrimanic character must be recognized.

The great Archangel Michael teaches us how such recognition can be made today if people are willing to listen to him. For the Michael schooling has worked on for millennia, and still today it is possible for us to draw near it. It teaches how Ahriman himself, as an author, made first attempts of a deeply shattering, deeply tragic character by working through a human being. Nietzsche's *Antichrist,* his *Ecce Homo,* his autobiography, and the annotations in *The Will to Power*—those most brilliant chapters of modern authorship with their often satanic content—were all written by Ahriman. In the art of printing he can exercise his sovereignty and inspire and impel his words, his thoughts onto paper. Ahriman has already begun to appear as an author and his work will continue in increasing number. We are called upon to become increasingly alert to this powerful new source of inspiration in order that we become able to recognize its source. Works written by human beings will certainly continue to appear, but we must be aware that a Being is honing his skills to become one of the most brilliant authors in our time: that Being is Ahriman. Human hands will write the works, but Ahriman will be the author. Just as the Evangelists of old were inspired by supersensible beings and wrote down their works through this inspiration, the works of Ahriman are being written by human beings today.

Every effort must be made to propagate, within the earthly realm, what was once taught by Michael in supersensible schools to souls predestined to receive it. Members of the Anthroposophical Society in particular are called upon by Rudolf Steiner to carry on this work.[12] The Anthroposophical Society was founded in Switzerland to pursue the subject of spiritual science, and Steiner was speaking to an anthroposophic audience when he made these comments. Indeed, since Steiner's time much has been written by Ahriman. His influence has become quite pervasive as we shall see.

One task of anthroposophers is to steadfastly cultivate the wisdom of the Archangel Michael, to bring courageous hearts to this Michaelic wisdom and to the realization that the first penetration of the earthly intelligence by the spiritual sword of Michael is when this sword is wielded by those individuals whose hearts have been penetrated by Michaelic wisdom. Thus a picture of Michael in a new form may inspire all of us—Michael standing within our human hearts and, beneath his feet, all the works authored by ahrimanic inspiration. Such an image need not be painted outwardly, as it was during the middle ages. In those days, the artists often portrayed the Dominican Scholastics above, with the books of heathen wisdom crushed under their feet. Today we need this other spiritual picture—devotion to Michael as he enters the world, laying hold of the intelligence upon Earth. To avoid being dazzled by Ahriman, we need constant alertness with regard to his brilliant works as an author. Ahriman will write his works in strange places, Steiner tells us, but they will definitely manifest. He is preparing many of his pupils for this sinister purpose. And now, in the twenty-first century, he has already been using the major media—television, films, computer programs, and such—to propagate his ideas in the major fields of human interest: philosophy, science, poetry, theology, drama, medicine, law, and sociology, to name a few. Ahriman will have become an author in all these domains according to spiritual investigation. And in all these spheres, watchfulness will be needed, along with reverent enthusiasm for Michaelic wisdom.

Human hearts must become the helpers of Michael in the conquering of the intelligence that has fallen to Earth. Just as the old Serpent was once destined to be crushed by Michael, the intelligence that has now become serpent-like must be re-spiritualized and conquered by the Michael forces in our hearts. And whenever the Serpent appears in its ahrimanic, unspiritualized state, it must be recognized through the alertness which can be developed through a Michael-like tenor of soul (Ibid.). This is why getting together in groups to study and discuss spiritual scientific findings is so important—face-to-face meeting, in person. That way the spirit of each individual is present in the room. This cannot be accomplished by any means other than person-to-person contact. Least of all can it be accomplished by electronic (read ahrimanic) means of communication. In the context of study, there are two laws of spiritual investigation which are little understood. They are enforced by the Masters of Wisdom and Harmonious Feeling to bring people together here on the physical plane of consciousness and activity.

People often ask: Well, why should I study spiritual matters while here on Earth? Why not wait until after I've died? Then I'll be in the spiritual world and will be able to see everything for myself anyway. The fact is that, unless people make the effort while here on Earth to understand spiritual matters through study, discussion, worship, and/or meditation, they will be unable to comprehend what they see in the spiritual worlds after death. The second, related law states that once certain areas of spiritual investigation have been disclosed by an investigator in physical terms, those areas may well become "off limits" to further investigation by others, even those with advanced faculties of perception, at least until these secondary investigators have read or heard about them and actively thought about them while here on the material level of consciousness. In this way even the printed word, which is of purely ahrimanic origin, can be used to a higher purpose.

Where would we find examples of Ahriman's writing today? Well, for starters, we could look in places where truth is distorted or where only partial pictures are presented. A good example would be the many articles that attack homeopathic medicine or acupuncture, healing modalities that work, but in such a way that they cannot be explained by the current theories of conventional, materialistic chemistry and medicine. It is therefore much more comfortable to just ignore such methods or dismiss them altogether as quackery or pseudo-science. Another example can be found in the study of correspondences between the stars or planets and human behavior. If it weren't so tragic, it would be amusing to see how so many of today's 'leading thinkers' refuse even to look at such phenomena, or, when they condescend to examine someone else's research along such lines, to ruthlessly distort such work in order to condemn it (see appendix I).

To help us see the qualities of the luciferic and ahrimanic realms, the following table may be of some assistance. The indications given here are not intended to be definitive, but rather are intended for further study and contemplation.

AHRIMANIC	LUCIFERIC
arrogance	pride
deceit, lies	illusions (of grandeur, etc.)
reductionist thinking	broad, sweeping generalities
control over others	indifference to others
everything that can be weighed, counted and measured	flighty, dreamy artistic imaginations
cold, calculating thought	voluptuousness, sensuality
materialistic science	sweeping social programs with little attention to human consequenses or fine details
conservatism	liberalism
the "nitty gritty"	the "airy-fairy"
THE ECONOMIC SPHERE	THE CULTURAL SPHERE

Without putting too fine a point on these differences, they can help us feel our way toward the qualities inherent in these two individualities and their legions of followers. Later we will look at a few examples of what may well be ahrimanically inspired works written during the past two decades or so. As well, we will take a closer look at what we mean by the above references to the economic and cultural spheres.

Five thousand years ago, dreamily pulling us into the glorious "golden age" of the past—that is Lucifer. Today, five thousand years later and rushing us forward into a cold, lifeless, and materialistic world order of the future—Ahriman. But Ahriman's world order, from a human perspective, would be a prison, pervaded by lies, ugliness and deceit. While Lucifer's great "golden age" of the past was indebted, in part, to dimensions of pure illusion. These are our two great enemy/friends, each offering us potentially great gifts, but each wanting to steer human evolution into very divergent directions and away from the proper and divinely ordained course intended for us. Humanity, all that is truly human, holds the balance, the equipoise between these two mighty, inimical forces. The question, of course, remains: What does it mean to be truly human?

Chapter Three

A Holoscopic Look at the Human Being

> "What luck for the rulers
> that people do not think!"
> —Adolf Hitler

WE MUST NOW attempt to gain a deeper understanding of ourselves as human beings, and our capacity for understanding (and misunderstanding), before we can hope to find a cure for the evils besetting us. Let's begin by examining this *mysterium magnum*, the human being, from a holoscopic perspective. First, however, since holoscopy, so far as I know, is a new term, we need to become more familiar with it and with some of the instruments or tools it proposes to place at our disposal.

Holoscopy shuns definitions. The minute you define something, you have circumscribed it with a shell and separated what it is from what it isn't. It therefore has no room for growth. It becomes perhaps more easily grasped by today's objective and reductionist consciousness, but we're left with a dead concept. Holoscopy attempts to transcend these limitations by portraying in an artistic, living way, rather than by defining. The following is a brief attempt to portray, or at least sketch, holoscopy itself. The few quotations from the *Oxford English Dictionary* (OED) should therefore be seen not as definitions, but as portraits or indications of the terrain.

Holoscopy is intended as an introduction to a science of the spirit. It combines the Greek words *holos*, meaning "whole," with *skopos*, "vision," or "sight." The suffix "scope," as in *microscope, telescope,* and so on, implies exact seeing, precise observation, and detailed examination. Holoscopy seeks to embrace the best in the human mind by encouraging awe and wonder as tools for a deeper understanding of life's mysteries, seeking a vision of wisdom appropriate to our times. Another meaning of the word *scope* provides "room for exercise, opportunity, or liberty to act; free course or play."

The English word *scope* warrants almost a full page in the OED, including: "the distance to which the mind reaches in its activities or purpose; reach or range of mental activity; extent of view, outlook or survey." Thus the vision of holoscopy remains open-ended. In philosophy, holism is concerned with the differences, for example, between organic and inorganic entities—the theory that an object or being has an identity other than, and exceeding, the sum of its inherent parts. Holoscopy incorporates holistic thinking, but it is not the opposite of reductionist thinking, as is holism. Rather, it incorporates both modes, holism and reductionism, as the situation demands. But these are not its only tools.

Holoscopy is inspired by Steiner's and Aurobindo's concepts of the various stages of consciousness higher than that of our normal, everyday mode of thought. It is also inspired by Goethe, whose method of scientific investigation is not only thoughtful, but also artistic, active, and contemplative. As holoscopists, we ourselves become the instruments of investigation; we become the "holoscope," if you will. As such, we must be at home with contemporary exactitude, precision and detail without losing our sense of awe and *reverence for the truth*, which is one of our greatest holoscopic investigative tools. Let's see if we can use this and other tools to gain a deeper insight into what it means to be a human being.

The ancient exhortation "Man, know thyself!" asks for a solution to one of the greatest riddles of the universe. Until now we have been looking at a polarity of two extremes, a duality. But we are not dualistic beings; in our inner nature; we are threefold. Our inner soul activity, leaving aside perception in this instance, which is a surface activity, consists of thinking, feeling, and willing. Sri Aurobindo's teachings of his integral, or synthetic, yoga made great strides in developing and balancing these three soul functions by combining the main streams of yoga, those of jnana yoga (spiritual knowledge), bhakti yoga (devotion) and karma yoga (selfless action), into one integrated whole. The path to true self-knowledge may best begin with a brief discussion of thinking, feeling, and willing, the three soul-powers which Aurobindo so masterfully brought into balance and perspective with his integral yoga.

Of these three, we are most awake in our thinking, or at least we should be. Spiritual science thus speaks to this faculty in us if we choose to become its students. If we were to be taught by means of emotional pleas to our feeling nature, we would doubtless feel manipulated. We wouldn't be free to accept or reject the teaching in full consciousness. We would be little more than sheep being led around by a manipulative crook at the neck. Yet thinking, *real thinking*, is an act of will. It takes real concentration to stick with a mental problem until it is solved. We sometimes hear of people who tell us that they have no control over their thoughts. This is a pathological condition and may indicate that those individuals have not put enough effort or discipline into their thinking. Once again, they choose by default to remain as sheep, in a kind of proto-human condition, easily swayed, easily duped, and, more germane to our subject, easily manipulated.

It is our duty to learn to think clearly if we hope to advance our human condition and overcome the threat of evil. The study of mathematics is an excellent beginning. In math we are already dealing with the supersensible world. There's no such thing as a one or a two in the physical world. This is why Ahriman gloats with glee when he sees us introduce calculators and computers into the primary grades of our schools. Even at the secondary level they should be used with extreme caution, if at all. My theory about children using computers, calculators, and television is very simple, if perhaps a bit idealistic: Fine, let them use these Ahrimanic devices all they want; provided they first understand thoroughly the principles behind them—the Boolean algebra, the logic gates, the schematics of television transmitters and receivers, and so on.

Then, once they construct their own simple computer, or at least assemble a more complex one from a kit, only then should they be free to use them. Otherwise these devices remain mysterious little boxes, little ahrimanic gods, which they "worship" every time they turn them on and stare at them without understanding their inner workings. Just look at all the time they devote (from devotion = worship) to these contraptions.

Still, *what* children watch is more important than whether they watch. Interactive TV and violent computer games and movies are the subject of *Stop Teaching Our Kids to Kill,* by Lt. Col. Dave Grossman and Gloria DeGaetano.[1] These two astute authors cite case after case of violence-addicted kids almost routinely killing others mostly, they claim, because they see such violence every day in the media and computer games they play for hours on end.[2] Marie Winn speaks of television as a drug in her book *The Plug-In Drug: Television, Computers, and Family Life,* which advocates strongly that parents take a much greater interest in the effects of this insidious cyclops of a babysitter.[3] The evidence is mounting that TV and computer games can have a strong deleterious, even pernicious, effect on our children.

We shouldn't be "against" these wonderful contraptions, which would mean simply acting like the destructive nineteenth century Luddites, who caused so much damage by rioting against the construction of textile mills in England. These devices, which are well worth studying and mastering, are already part of our lives; we can't turn our backs on them. That would mean closing ourselves off to a part of the world that already exists. Rather, we should understand them and become masters of their technology. That's probably the best way to free ourselves from their subtle but powerful influences in our lives. This is part of what it means to be truly human—to become increasingly and consciously aware of the world around us. This we do through our thinking, our faculties of comprehension and reason.

On the other hand, if we accept the task of studying these devices as some kind of boring duty or stringent obligation, without being able to bring enthusiasm to our task, then perhaps we are better leaving them uncomprehended. To study in such a fashion leads us again into

Ahriman's realm. We cannot defeat Ahriman without generating a bit of Luciferic enthusiasm in ourselves. Consider the countless number of people who punch a time-clock every work-day at some dull, grey factory to work on an endlessly repetitive assembly line. We don't have to be seers or initiates to see at least part of the damage this does to their souls. All we have to do is to imaginatively enter into the phenomena of our times in a holoscopic fashion, to think about them reflectively and without prejudice, to see a little deeper into their reality. And the reality we see in such cases is quite disturbing indeed.

How important to us is our thinking? Extremely so; thinking is the new clairvoyance. Both Steiner and Aurobindo call for the development of successive stages of higher cognition. In 1894, while still in his early thirties, Rudolf Steiner published one of the most monumental works of his entire career, *Die Philosophie der Freiheit* (*The Philosophy of Freedom*).[4] When read carefully, this work guides students to a perception of themselves as free "I" beings in the spiritual worlds, a perception of the potential for true freedom. Although Steiner's Ph.D. thesis was concerned primarily with epistemology (a study or theory of knowledge), he was able to write this book in clear, nontechnical language. His stirring call for a sense-free thinking could be seen as a major theme weaving throughout his entire adult life. Holoscopy is one approach to such transcendent thinking by helping us become aware of the mode of our thinking at any particular time. But Steiner approaches the question from another perspective, too. He advocates a more meditative approach. For example, he suggests contemplation of the saying "Wisdom lives in the light." Now from a purely physical perspective, this expression is meaningless. But by practicing it regularly for just a few minutes a day we begin to feel that we are on the right path. Unlike ordinary thinking, which is "brain bound," contemplating "wisdom lives in the light" frees our thinking from the brain. We do not tire so easily with this practice as we may do with ordinary thought processes.[5]

How far can ordinary thinking take us? Not very far. For example, idealists insist that the Earth will become a paradise if only idealism gains the upper hand. Materialists feel the same way about materialism, as do socialists about their world view and liberals and conservatives about theirs. This is all incredibly naïve. Why? Because all these views have their own validity and verity. From a higher, let's call it a "spiritual," perspective, each of these habits of thought has a kernel of truth. Most people who make the effort to really think can penetrate to this higher spiritual reality where all world views have their proper place.

These days, we pride ourselves in our thinking, yet actually know very little about what true thinking is. We must engender in ourselves a lively interest in the spiritual worlds through our thinking if we can hope to progress with morality as far as we have with mere intellectuality. We must gain the ability to behold the spiritual forces and impulses that surge everywhere through our world. But it is uncomfortable to think, to really think. And it is very easy to asume that by simply rearranging our biases we have produced an original thought. True thinking is an act of will, and by its means we become able to experience the spiritual world as a reality. This leads us of necessity to develop something else that has suffered such decline during the past centuries of materialism: namely, an inner sense of responsibility.[6]

So many books and articles have been written about Steiner's observations and practice of thinking that interested readers should have little difficulty in pursuing their studies of this fundamentally important subject further.

What Steiner calls Sense-free thinking Aurobindo refers to as "higher mind." It is the next level above our ordinary day-to-day consciousness. Of it he says in his own inimitable style:

> Our first decisive step out of our human intelligence, our normal mentality, is an ascent into a higher Mind, a mind no longer of mingled light and obscurity or half light, but a large clarity of the spirit. Its basic substance is a unitarian sense of being with a powerful multiple dynamization capable of the formation of a multitude of aspects of knowledge, ways of action, forms and significances of becoming, of all of which there is a spontaneous inherent knowledge.... It is a luminous thought mind, a mind

of spirit-born conceptual knowledge. An all-awareness emerging from the original identity, carrying the truths the identity held in itself, conceiving swiftly, victoriously, multitudinously, formulating and by self-power of the idea effectually realizing its conceptions, is the character of this greater mind of knowledge. But here, in this greater thought, there is no need of seeking and self-critical ratiocination, no logical motion step by step towards a conclusion, no mechanism of express or implied deductions and inferences, no building or deliberate concatenation of idea with idea in order to arrive at an ordered sum or outcome of knowledge.... This higher consciousness is knowledge, formulating itself on a basis of self-existent all-awareness and manifesting some part of its integrality, a harmony of its significances put into thought form. It can freely express itself in single ideas, but its most characteristic movement is a mass ideation, a system or totality of seeing truth at a single view; the relations of idea with idea, of truth with truth are not established by logic but preexist and emerge already self-seen in the integral whole. There is an initiation into forms of an ever-present but, until now, inactive knowledge, not a system of conclusions from premises or data; this thought is a self-revelation of eternal wisdom, not acquired knowledge.[7]

Both Steiner and Aurobindo describe three yet higher stages of thinking or cognition but, since discussing them here would take us into the realms of initiation itself, they are best left for now on the other side of the fence surrounding the field we are here attempting to plough; limiting ourselves by choice to our holoscopic implements. The next inner soul activity we will look at, though far more briefly than our look at thinking, is that of *feeling*.

The level of consciousness in our feeling can be compared to that of dreamy sleep. We are but semi-conscious in this activity. For many people, feelings approach them like beasts in the wild. They have no control over them. For others the animals are tamed and friendly, totally under the control of their owner. We will soon discuss the six exercises

Steiner gave us, designed to powerfully heal all three soul functions, thinking, feeling and willing, which can help us control them in a more balanced and harmonious way.

In our willing, or volition, we are in deep, dreamless sleep. When I raise a spoonful of cereal to my mouth I am not aware of all the muscles, tendons, and tissues involved in performing this act. I just do it. Less conscious am I of the act of chewing, or of the remarkably fluid movements of the tongue as it tests and tastes the food, then selflessly assists the teeth in the act of chewing and, later, in cleaning up the debris. Such great wisdom operates through our will, because it's the divine spiritual beings of the celestial hierarchies operating in us. We as human beings are a microcosm of the entire universe, and as such are worthy of a far deeper study than we can hope to accomplish here. As threefold beings, our thinking is centered in our nerve and sensory organism—the head, spinal column, and nerves that permeate the human body. The rhythmic system operates in our feelings: the heart and lungs and the blood circulating throughout the system. The will finds its focus in our metabolic and limb organism. What a valuable discovery Steiner made when he perceived this remarkable threefold nature of the human being, with their three respective foci in the physical body. He presents a picture worthy of serious contemplation, although he was certainly not the first to see the tripartite human being. Twenty-five hundred years ago, Confucius made the following observation in his *Analects:* "The way of the superior human is threefold, but I am not equal to it. Virtuous, he is free from anxieties; wise, he is free from perplexities; bold, he is free from fear."[8]

Spiritual science always leaves us free. Each of us has to decide whether or not we will pursue it and thus begin the long, hard, but never tedious ascent toward the control of one's destiny. We can accept this gift of a deeper picture of the human being, perhaps without understanding it at first, but with the intention of musing over it from time to time; or we can refuse the gift altogether. Our loss. The holoscopist could be called almost greedy in this respect. She is endlessly curious, accepting such gifts wherever they may be found, so she can further adorn the walls of her richly endowed mental amusement area.

Rudolf Steiner's Six Exercises

The following exercises appear, with minor variations, in several of Steiner's works.[9] Their purpose is to strengthen and balance the development of the three soul forces described above. Presented here in a simplified form, they are the first steps to self mastery, and carry a strong healing power, both necessary attributes for the successful overcoming of evil. They are each intended to be done for at least a month before adding the next. Also, it is best to do them in the order given. One could but wonder what kind of a world this would be if people spent half the energy on these exercises that they spend on developing their physical bodies. After all, exercise cycles don't take us anywhere. The fruits of our efforts in soul development, however, take us into a far richer and more meaningful future. Furthermore, they engender valuable soul qualities that will assist us greatly in future incarnations. The parable of the talents has deep significance in this regard.

1. Control of Thinking: For five minutes each day concentrate on a simple, everyday object, the simpler the better: a paper clip, wooden pencil, or hairpin are good for starters. The idea is to keep your mind focused on the object itself: How is it made? What is it made of? Why is it designed the way it is? Don't use anything to which you are emotionally attached. Initially you may need the actual object in front of you to assist in concentrating, but it is better to try to picture it in your mind's eye without external support. After a month of this, if successful, add the second exercise.

2. Initiative of Action: The purpose of this exercise is to do something each day from your own initiative, something that the outer press of circumstances has no influence over. Some people start out with a simple act like moving their comb from one pocket to another, or turning a ring around on their finger. Try to do this at the same time each day. Then, as you progress, the act can become more complex. As an example of the health-promoting qualities of these exercises, people who have impaired their will forces through substance abuse should find this exercise particularly valuable in helping them become more productive members of society.

3. *Rising above Pleasure and Pain:* We all have cycles of pleasure and pain, joy and sorrow. The idea here is a little difficult to describe; you choose when and how to express these feelings rather than let the feelings express themselves through you. The difference is subtle, yet with perseverance it will be seen that there is a big difference between my joy taking control of me and my assuming control of my joy. The same applies to sorrow and all other emotions—rage, passions, and so on. Rather than depleting us of feelings, this exercise enriches them and contributes immensely to our mental hygiene.

4. *Maintaining a Positive Attitude:* In every evil act there is hidden somewhere a small kernel of good, in every evil man, a spark of the divine. The object of this exercise is to look for and find that kernel, that spark. This has nothing to do with seeing evil as good or black as white. Rather, it entails a focus on the good.

5. *Openness:* Many of us restrict ourselves from any further growth by closing our minds to anything new, unheard of, or never tried before. This is almost an automatic response with some people. However ridiculous or impossible-sounding something may seem when we first hear it, this exercise calls for us to keep at least a small niche open in our mind where we say to ourselves; well, it may be. I'll have to check it out. Steiner is not advocating here that we become gullible and accept everything. By no means; rather, the intent here is not to dismiss anything without first carefully examining it. After doing this exercise for a while, you may start feeling appalled at the number of people who are quite predictable in their opinions. Liberals as liberals, conservatives as conservatives; whatever their bent may be, you become more aware of how totally devoid of true thinking they really are. Some may be very clever at expressing their ideas, but if those ideas stem from any predisposition toward one stance or another, you can be sure they are not really thinking. However, we must be aware that it is all too easy to

become judgmental in this regard. Holoscopic individuals are far more interested in finding and correcting flaws in their own thinking than in the thinking of others.

6. *Equilibrium:* The intent is that we don't allow any of the attributes gained by the previous five exercises to slip away. Review them all in the proper order. See where additional work may be needed. Keep them in balance and harmony. In short, continue to repeat all five exercises systematically and in regular rotation. Steiner goes so far as to say that the six exercises just described will paralyze the possible harmful influence of other esoteric exercises, leaving only the benefits. In addition, they can assure that our meditation and concentration efforts will yield positive results. The esotericist must not be satisfied with fulfilling the demands of conventional morality, no matter how conscientiously, because this kind of morality becomes very egotistical if you say such things as, "I want to be good so I will be thought good by others." Esotericists do not do what is good simply because they want to be thought of as good. Rather, they gradually learn to recognize that the good alone furthers evolution, and that evil and foolishness and ugliness lay obstacles in its path.[10]

We will now look at people as *social* beings, how we interact with one another in our various spheres of activity. Here we see a new threefold organization, what Steiner calls the threefold social organism. Once again, all we can present are mere sketches, leaving it to the serious student to bring them to life in his or her consciousness through further study and contemplation. There are many works by Steiner and others that explore this social threefold nature in rich and productive ways. As we shall see, the nature of this threefold quality in society is quite different from that found in the individual human being.

When we attempt to make some order in our minds of the wide scope of human interaction, we are eventually led to see three major nexus of activity, three scopes of human endeavor. The first of these Steiner names the *cultural sphere.* In it are all the aspirations that provide a leavening or a buoyant force for civilization: education, the arts, entertainment, and religion, among other impulses, all live here. These liberating forces uplift us and give us a direction and a purpose in life. The keyword here is *freedom*. We are, or should be, free to choose which schools we send our children to, which churches we worship in, and whichever works of art we want in our homes; as well as a free selection in the choice of concerts and any other cultural activities. Composers and other artists, too, should be free to create provided, of course, that their creations don't impinge on the rights of others.

This brings us to the second sphere, the sphere of *human rights*. Here we are concerned, not with culture and the arts, but rather with the art of living together with other human beings without disturbing them. The US Declaration of Independence states: "We hold these truths to be self-evident, that all men are created equal." Taken alone, this is absurd; some are born with no arms or legs, or with severe mental or perceptual handicaps. But it answers this objection with "that they are endowed by their Creator with certain unalienable Rights, that among these are Life, Liberty, and the pursuit of Happiness." Now we see it. We are born with *equal rights*, thus leading us to the ideal; the keyword for this sphere is obviously *equality*. In an ideal world, the poorest of the poor would have the same human rights as the doctor, the lawyer, and the senator. *Equality*.

The third sphere of human activity has to do with how we feed, clothe, and shelter ourselves, how we interact, not with the spirit of the cultural sphere, nor with other human beings as in the rights sphere, but with the Earth. It is the sphere of *economics*. In this realm, we are concerned with all the products and services we supply for others through our work, how we manufacture, refine, and alter the products of the Earth, then circulate them to satisfy the needs of our fellow human beings. The keyword here is *companionship*, or "brotherhood," as Steiner calls it, working together in associations for the common good.

Freedom, equality, brotherhood, the well-known *Liberté, Égalité, Fraternité* of the French Revolution and the "Declaration of the Rights of Man." These powerful revolutionary concepts now take on a more viable and practical meaning when we see them applied to their proper spheres of human activity. Otherwise they remain as self-contradictory, empty ideals. For how can you have, for example, both freedom and equality if they aren't properly circumscribed? One person's freedom would likely impose on another's equality. It is thanks to the deep, penetrating genius of Rudolf Steiner that we can now see this powerful slogan in its true light. It is not one slogan, but three stirring key-words for three very different worlds of human endeavor. *Liberté* opening up the cultural sphere to freedom and light; *Egalité*, with its promise of equal rights for everybody; and *Fraternité*, the harmonious working together of manufacturer, wholesaler, retailer, and customer in companionship and mutual trust.

"But those are just ideals," one might say; "they don't exist in the real world." Ah, but they do exist. It's just that these three spheres of social life are so intermingled that they, as well as the forces and laws pertaining to them, are dangerously confused. Yet the whole of human history consists of struggles to extricate and separate them. Think of the so-called divine right of kings or the tremendous power wielded in both the cultural and rights spheres by the land barons. Think, too, of the immense power of the churches in both the political and economic spheres. In prehistoric times this was not a problem. Now it should be one of our primary concerns. President Eisenhower had an inkling of this danger when he warned, in his farewell address, against what he called the military-industrial complex as well as the dangers of big government. What he didn't say, however, was that not only has the legal or rights sphere, the government, become too entangled with the economic sphere, but also that the cultural sphere has been left totally out in the cold. There is no balance.

Though her book appeared a year before the Campaign Finance Reform Act of 2002, Elizabeth Drew's *The Corruption of American Politics: What Went Wrong and Why*, contains a wealth of material relevant to this question. Her indictment of Washington politics is strong, using such phrases as "the self-centered, short-sighted, limited-vision, reactive politics of today." [11] She makes a compelling case for the separation of at least the economic and human rights spheres. The implications of this concept are far-reaching, and a thorough understanding of the threefold social organism would take us a long way from many of the ills that beset society today. Fortunately, there is a growing number of excellent books that treat the manifold aspects of this fascinating and fundamentally important concept.

In the United States, members of the Senate and the House of Representatives were going through torturous and painful recriminations and self-examinations prior to passing the new campaign finance reform bill. Sadly, in that bill as it was finally passed there was no limit placed on the amount of "soft money" that could be contributed to the various parties. Soft money consists of those contributions that are earmarked (supposedly) for the party or other organization so long as it does not advocate overtly an individual candidate. The result is that hundreds of thousands of dollars, sometimes millions, change hands and the politicians are placed in a position where almost overpowering forces of coercion are involved in just about every major bill they write. The net result is that the Political Action Committees (PACs) that contribute to this madness are, for all practical purposes, writing the laws that control our destiny. It is therefore the PACs who are really running our country, and far too many politicians have simply become their puppets. Democracy has become little more than a myth believed in by those who refuse to carefully observe its processes by means of tested alternative media, and then think for themselves. In an ideal world (one can dream) it would be a felony for any politician or party to accept more than a cup of coffee from any organization or individual. Politicians would thus be free to listen to the arguments of their constituents, not impeded or tempted in any way by the powerful forces of coercion and greed. In such an ideal world a great onus of responsibility would be placed upon the media to provide free and equal time to all viable candidates and parties. And the media themselves would also have to be untainted. Yet the mainstream media, even many so-called "public" broadcasters, have sold out to the highest bidder, the same high-rollers behind all the obscene PAC money just discussed. Years ago there were strict limits to the number of radio and TV stations an individual or group could own in any given market, but those days are long gone. Wouldn't it be nice if the government resisted the temptations of the media millions, and reinstated those restrictions? Control of the media would then fall back into the hands of local people rather than those of the huge, greedy media giants. Well, it doesn't hurt to dream a little.

What happens when the heavy hand of government takes over and makes decisions that more properly belong to the business or economic sphere? We get absurdities such as the government designing our toilets. The Energy Policy and Conservation Act of 1992 dictates that all toilets installed in this country use no more than 1.6 gallons of water, regardless of the fact that you may have to flush three or four times to get them to complete their job. All this happens simply because some states have a water shortage. This is a regional problem, not one for the insensitive federal government.

And where does all this leave the arts, the cultural sphere? It is left out in the cold. The government has taken over the business of overseeing the education of our children—a business it has no right to be in, with the net result that we have a strong tendency toward mediocrity and uniformity. The legitimate purview of the government is to assure that all parents have the right to send their children to the school of their choice. But the government has no right to meddle in the content of the curricula of those schools. The education minister or secretary of education, or whatever you want to call such bureaucrats, should be selected (if we need them at all) by educators themselves, and they should not have to answer to the government unless questions of human rights are involved. The government should have no say whatsoever in matters of content in the cultural sphere—matters of education, the arts, and religion. The government's legitimate role in these matters is solely in assuring that its citizens have the right to free choices when selecting schools, churches, artistic activities, and the like. This may be a difficult point for some to see at first, especially those who have a stake in the existing structure. But when this concept of the threefold social order is really thought through—that is, without the slightest prejudice—its beauty and wisdom becomes obvious. It will further be seen that a host of evils besetting our society, with all of its confused social policies, will almost automatically be eradicated once a healthy threefold society is inaugurated.

Business, government, and the arts (including education and religion)—the economic, human rights and cultural spheres—are equally important for a healthy, sane society. Just as we can prove to ourselves by thinking that the total of the inside angles of a triangle always equals 180 degrees, we can also "see" that the human social life is spiritually divided into three distinct spheres, and that the physical reality must reflect that spiritual reality before it can become whole and healthy. Anyone who is serious about reinventing government in a healthy, wholesome way should give serious consideration to the threefold social order. It is a reality that must be seen and implemented. All three spheres must be seen as free and independent of each other, and of equal importance.

The last five thousand years of recorded history consist of each of these three spheres trying to wrest itself free from the influence of the others. But this trend seems to be going in the wrong direction. The overwhelming incursion of the economic-monetary sphere into the decision making activities of the human rights sphere—the government—could be seen as a "mother crime." A term we use for those that spawn further crimes. This becomes particularly insidious when the media, which are supposed to report on such crimes, are controlled by the perpetrators themselves. Channels such as Free Speech TV (Channel 9415 on Dish Satellite TV) however, seem to be gaining some ground in the face of the media giants. It is extremely elucidating to compare stories carried on FSTV with those on its distant cousins, the widely-watched corporate media.

Anther mother crime is the criminalization of drug abuse, rather than treating drug addiction as a medical problem. This leads to endless crime and suffering and forces addicts to commit the most heinous crimes simply to support their habit. Illegal trafficking in drugs continues, despite the billions of dollars spent in the patently pointless "drug war." Still another mother crime is the deliberate use of the public relations industry to misinform the public about important issues that affect all of us. For a chilling wake-up call in this matter see, for instance, *Trust Us, We're Experts: How Industry Manipulates Science and Gambles with Your Future* by Sheldon Rampton and John Stauber.[12] Closely related to this, though dealing with a specific topic, is Alicia Mundy's *Dispensing with the Truth: The Victims, the Drug Companies, and the Dramatic Story Behind the Battle over Fen-phen*.[13] Both works are well written, thoroughly referenced, and will greatly assist the reader in seeing through the barrage of lies that poses as news in today's troubled world.

Fortunately, responsible editors are now beginning to warn their readers about the possibility of biases and unmentioned weaknesses in some of their published articles because of the pervasive influence of financially interested parties not only conducting the research and writing the articles, but also peer reviewing them. Dr Catherine DeAngelis, editor of the *Journal of the American Medical Association* (JAMA), for example, published several articles on this problem, the pursuit of which is beyond the scope of the present work, in the issue of June 2, 2002.[14] But such efforts at honesty should not go unnoticed—after all, without honest media where would we be?

To continue our holoscopic study of the human being we must enter the occult, or hidden areas of our being. These areas are hidden from physical sight, but they manifest outwardly in such a way that anyone with a healthy degree of human understanding and lack of prejudice can apprehend them in the "mind's eye." We look about us, and we see the mineral, the plant, and the animal kingdoms—and then we see the human being, who is as different from the animals as the animals are from the plants. We thus have four kingdoms, not three, as Ahriman would have us believe. Human beings are not animals, and we will soon see why as we look at ourselves holoscopically with the aid of spiritual scientific investigation.

When comparing the plant with the mineral world, it is not difficult to see that the plant has life. The stone, even a crystal, does not enjoy the benefits of life and has no lower kingdom from which to draw sustenance.

It cannot propagate itself as plants do. Occult investigation tells us that the plant has a "life body," sometimes called "the body of formative forces" or "etheric body." ("Ether" here is not to be confused with the hypothetical "luminiferous ether" postulated by nineteenth century physicists in an attempt to explain the transmission of electromagnetic waves.) Humans and animals, as well as plants, are alive; therefore they all have an etheric body. All four kingdoms have a physical body, but only plants, animals, and human beings have an etheric body. The form, or "gesture," of a plant is a physical expression of its etheric body, each species having a unique gesture in response to its environment. It is interesting to contemplate the various gestures of each plant species in an effort to come a little closer to its inner nature and to an awareness of its etheric body. This is what Goethe was able to accomplish in his botanical studies.[15]

Turning to the animals, we see that they have sentience and desire, qualities lacking in a plant. A cat is able to stalk a mouse before pouncing on it. Its physical body, indeed, the shape and form of all animals, is an expression of its astral body, sometimes called a soul. Some occultists call this the "desire body," but that is an incomplete term. *Astral* (star) is a more appropriate term, because the astral "substance" (another inadequate word) originates in the cosmos and in the stars themselves. Humans also, quite obviously, have an astral body. What, then, distinguishes humans from animals? Both have physical, etheric, and astral bodies. What is it that makes human beings human? It is eternal spirit.

When you say "I" to yourself, you are addressing a spiritual being unique in the entire universe. No other being anywhere in the universe can use that word as a mode of address to the same individuality as you. Animals cannot commit evil because they do not possess an individual I in the physical world; their I is a collective reality, hovering over them in the astral plane as a group soul. All animals of the same species have the same "I." It is not out of egoism that the English "I" is capitalized; it is the name of a god, albeit a nascent one in most cases. To say that we are gods, as Christ does in John 10:34 (see also Isaiah 41:23), is a far cry from what Lucifer promised while we were still in that wondrous, etheric realm called the Garden of Eden—the promise that we shall be *as* gods, knowing good from evil (Genesis 3:5). Yet, without Lucifer's promise of becoming god*like* we would never have had the possibility of meeting Christ on Earth, assuring us that *in potentia*, at lease, we *are* gods. In a later chapter we will examine briefly the central point of all earthly evolution—the great, unique Deed of Christ—which made this possible. In the meantime, we will look briefly a little closer (though as holoscopically as possible) at the four human bodies: physical, etheric, astral and "I." The study of what it means to be human is a very complex subject, and the best we can hope for in this present work are challenges for further study and contemplation.

In the physical world we are subject to the laws that pertain here: gravity, inertia, the need for physical hygiene, temperance, and so on; as children we learn to respect these laws. We also have certain needs on the physical plane that we don't have elsewhere; we have to eat. We also need clothing and shelter. It is interesting that in American slang during the early twentieth century the word commonly used for money, which buys all these things, was "dough." Somehow in the intervening years this dough got baked and emerged during the sixties as "bread." Bread has been called the staff of life. But, as we are reminded so succinctly, we do "not live by bread alone."

We were living in the etheric world before we were tempted to trespass into matter, to enter the physical plane. Our etheric bodies are the bearers of all our memories, as well as our fundamental temperaments, whether choleric, sanguine, phlegmatic, or melancholic, as the ancients referred to them. Here we have needs, too. We have the need of forgiveness. Yet we are only partially guilty of the fall of humanity, because, as we learned earlier, we were not fully conscious when we succumbed to that temptation. Therefore, we have the right to ask for forgiveness, but of course before we are qualified to do this we must first learn to forgive.

The astral world is filled with many temptations. Our astral body is the seat of all our desires, rages, and passions. We must seek purity, chastity, even holiness, if ever we expect to be led on a path of righteousness.

The old adage "Sticks and stones may break my bones, but names will never hurt me" is a misstatement regarding the astral plane; in this realm even our thoughts have power. Rudolf Steiner warns us that a thought of rage or revenge on the physical plane produces results on the astral plane that can inflict great harm to the individual concerned. When we succumb to the temptation of telling a lie, it is actually a murder on the astral plane. It is even worse, Steiner tells us, than a physical murder. How can we overcome these great temptations? We must focus on the good, the beautiful, and the true—all that ennobles us as human beings. The temptations are there; we have to find the divine leadership away from them.

As we mentioned earlier, an animal cannot commit evil because it does not have an "I" on the physical plane. The French word *je*, the German *ich* (J-Ch) and the English *I* (J in the old script) all signify one thing: Jesus Christ. He is the spark of divinity within each of us. Paul was quite right when, in his letter to the Galatians, he said, "I live; yet not I, but Christ lives in me" (Galatians 2:20). Paul could say this because he was initiated by Christ into the mysteries of the spirit. For the rest of us it is enough to know that Christ is present, waiting to be resurrected in us, in our thoughts, our feelings, and our actions. True, in our "I" we are capable of evil. Yet, such works as Shakespeare's great dramas, Wagner's epic operas, and the magnificent Gothic cathedrals—in fact all of our great accomplishments as human beings—are the outer manifestations of our indomitable spirit, our eternal "I," often with the help of inspiration from above. It is with our "I" that we have the capacity to encompass the range of the entire great vertical polarity of evil discussed earlier, from the depths of Ahriman at the base, to the soaring heights of Lucifer's pride-filled expanses at the top. It is for this reason, too, that in reference to the "I" we may ask: Deliver us from the evil (ones).

Christ was both describing and speaking to the four members of the human being when he taught the four "us" petitions of the Lord's Prayer, which we have just attempted to approach, with all reverence, in a holoscopic manner; that is, from the human perspective with our current level of consciousness. But it must be recognized that a successful holoscopic examination of these great words would not have been possible without the guidance and spiritual investigations of Rudolf Steiner. It is only with the deepest humility, reverence, and gratitude that we can stand in the presence of this mighty prayer now that one of its veils has been lifted.[16] And we are grateful, too, to the countless biblical scholars who have spent many years of diligent research in an effort to fathom, from the physical plane, the deep meanings of this great universal-human prayer. And we are grateful to the millions of devout souls who have used this prayer through the centuries in their daily meditations. All these efforts from the human side produce their results from the spiritual and have now made these gifts of a deeper understanding possible.

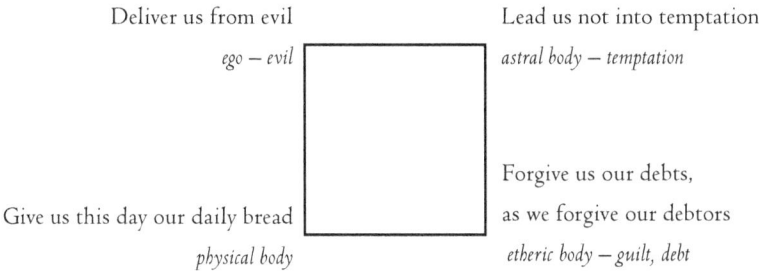

In the table, spirit self, life spirit, and spirit human refer to future conditions of the astral, etheric, and physical bodies, respectively, once they have become completely purified and cleansed of all imperfection. As such, these bodies are, for most of us, still in the spirit worlds awaiting our work of preparation and purification.

Next we must gather the courage to look at an aspect of humanity that may place us in a position to become an easy mark for scorn and ridicule from the many sardonic pedants of our day, namely, a discussion of *demons, ghosts,* and *phantoms*. No comprehensive discussion of evil, even an introductory work such as this, can ignore them. The Gospels are full of references to Christ casting out demons, and yet most of us don't see them. How do such entities come into being?

My almost violent response (see chapter I) when I first encountered Steiner's works was not simply *my* response, but that of the demons in me. They prompted me to throw down the book and storm out of the room. When I picked up my first book on Steiner's spiritual science, those demons met their match, and they knew it. Of course, I must still assume responsibility for all that I think and do. This is another reason why Rudolf Steiner never became the most famous man of the twentieth century; the demons in some of us react with terror when his name is mentioned and continue all manner of hindrances and excuses in an attempt to prevent us from studying his work.

I've seen people who had never heard of Steiner or Anthroposophy recoil when those names were mentioned in conversation. "It just doesn't feel right" is another response after reading just a few pages. Many people, when they begin to practice the six exercises discussed here, suddenly find a hundred reasons why they shouldn't be done at that particular time. To the holoscopist this can be seen as a further indication of their validity and effectiveness. They require intense, inner work. Of course they 'just don't feel right' to one who loves sloth and ease, or to the demons we may harbor and whose very existence is imperiled by regular practice. Steiner's exercises in concentration and meditation (particularly those in his seminal work *How to Know Higher Worlds*) are designed to rid us of those foul, ahrimanic entities. In a 1908 lecture course, *The Influence of Spiritual Beings upon Man*, Steiner introduced his audience to three categories of demon-like entities (phantoms; ghosts, or specters; and demons). He stressed the importance of becoming aware of them and that such knowledge can become a useful basis for completely improving our soul's health when we take it to heart.

He starts by reminding us that, in the astral world, a lie—even when we only think it—is a kind of murder that "has a far more devastating effect for that world than any misfortune in the physical world." *Lying*, however, should not be thought of in the way we normally conceive of the term. From a spiritual scientific perspective, any coloration of the truth, say, for purposes of convention or of party considerations, is considered a lie. In other words, the threshold of what constitutes a lie is much lower than is generally thought. In many respects, our whole lives are saturated, perhaps not with lies but with manifestations bearing untruthful coloring. Nevertheless, from a spiritual scientific perspective, such instances must be considered lies because they have the same effect in the astral body. What is that effect?

We will continue with this question, but first, it is necessary to further clarify the roles of our various bodies when we sleep. During sleep the "I" and astral body leave the physical and etheric bodies behind in the bed. In this state, the bodies left behind need to be maintained by cosmic beings from higher planes, otherwise we would become too plant-like when we sleep; the sleeper would have only a physical body and an etheric body, just like a plant. These lofty angelic beings work as our surrogate I and astral body during sleep, and as a result we feel regenerated and refreshed when we awake. It is for this reason, too, that spiritual scientists approach sleep with a mood of reverent gratitude to those beings for protecting and helping us while we are asleep. (Sleep is distinguished from death by the fact that in death our etheric body, together with the astral body and "I," leaves the physical body behind. This is why sleep is sometimes referred to as the "little brother of death.")

The spiritual investigator tells us that when we indulge in lies—that is, when a person has told a lie during the day—its effect remains in the physical body and can be seen by clairvoyant perception while the person sleeps. Suppose this individual is altogether untruthful and piles up many lies during the day. In this case, there will be many of these effects in the physical body. These supersensible packets of lies tend to harden and become enclosures that become disagreeable to the beings of higher worlds who must take possession of the physical body during the night and who carry out the functions otherwise exercised by our own astral body and "I" during the day. The result is that, in the course of life and because the body is "diseased" with these packets of lies, portions of those higher beings who descend into the human physical and etheric bodies during the night become detached from those higher beings and are trapped, as it were, in the lie packets and infest the physical body for the rest of one's life. Then, later, when that host person dies, these detached portions of higher beings assume a life of their own and are released from the body. They form a class of elemental beings, related to our physical bodies, called "phantoms" by spiritual science. Such foul beings are conjured into the earthly realms through lies, calumnies, and slander, and they are free to flit and whir about in our world (or rather, in the astral world closest to our physical one) and contribute their mischief.

Not only the physical, but the etheric and astral bodies, too, have related elemental beings that we conjure up in various ways. In the case of the etheric body, they are called specters, or ghosts; they manifest through bad laws, unjust social orders, and anything that leads to lack of harmony among human beings. Rudolf Steiner directly beheld such entities and he reports that large numbers of people harbor them in their etheric bodies. To one who is able to see these things spiritually, "their physical bodies are crammed, one might say, with phantoms, and their etheric bodies are crammed with specters. And as a rule, after a person's death ... all this rises and disperses and populates the world."[17]

So there we have the second type of entity, created by our failings. The first category, phantoms, is created in the physical body by our mendacity, lying and deceit, whereas the second class, the specters, is created in the etheric body through unjust social orders or laws, by any social condition that leads to social disharmony.

The third category, the demons, is created in our astral bodies when we attempt to influence the thinking of others and overrule their minds.

In all that works from soul to soul in our world, from the giving of unjustifiable advice to all those methods that people employ in order to overwhelm others, in every act that does not allow the free soul to confront the free soul, but employs, even in the slightest degree, forcible means of convincing and persuasion, in all this, forces are working from soul to soul, which again so influence these souls that it is expressed in the night in the astral body. The astral body gets these 'enclosures' and thereby beings are detached from other worlds and whir through our world again as elemental beings. They belong to the class of demons. They exist solely because intolerance and oppression of thought have in various ways been used in our world. That is how these hosts of demons have arisen in our world.[18]

Is there anything we can do to quell the effects of these inimical beings? Surely it's one thing to become aware of them and how they are created, but it's quite another to effectively eradicate them or minimize their influence on our thinking, feeling, and behavior.

Prayer is a good beginning. "Prayer prepares us for mysticism, mysticism for meditation and concentration, and from that point we are directed to the real work of spiritual research."[19] But prayer, real prayer, has nothing to do with ordering God around or reminding him to take care of your relatives and friends, which is the general practice these days. Rather, prayer entails a submission to what the future may bring. The words uttered by Christ at Gethsemane could be seen as the quintessential Christian prayer: "Father, if possible let this cup (of suffering) pass; nevertheless, not mine, but Thy will be done."

Taking prayer a step further, we come to "deliverance," an effective method practiced in some Protestant churches. The Rev. Don Basham, a pioneer of deliverance, explains how he developed this method, as well as some of its wonderful results, in his very readable and worthwhile *Deliver Us from Evil: A Pastor's Reluctant Encounters with the Powers of Darkness*. Another recent work on this subject is Neal Lozano's *Unbound: a Practical Guide to Deliverance from Evil Spirits*, which, according to one review, promotes a gentler, safer method of purging these beings. The Roman Catholic counterpart of deliverance is "exorcism." For a fascinating, true account of an exorcism the reader is referred to *The Exorcist* by William Peter Blatty. Originally published as a novel, it was later revealed that this work was based on an actual case of demonic possession. So the novel, as well as the popular movie based on it, can be considered a fairly accurate depiction of an exorcism.

As mentioned, the various exercises in *How to Know Higher Worlds*, notably the six "preparatory exercises" discussed earlier in this chapter, have proven especially efficacious in controlling these entities. We must remember, however, that when Christ cast out demons, he always admonished the individual to "go and sin no more." This means that we should make every effort not to lie (phantoms), to avoid unjust social situations (specters), and not to impose one's will unjustly over another person (demons). I say "unjustly" because, when rearing children, for example, such impositions are occasionally needed. The creation of these entities has far-reaching karmic consequences, a topic we will discuss later.

Should we be held responsible for any acts prompted by such foul beings operating in us? This is an interesting question, with manifold legal and ethical ramifications. Consider: If I were to build a house using slipshod methods and inferior materials, should I be held responsible if it collapses three years later? It seems that unless we continually try to take more responsibility than we can handle, unless we constantly stretch ourselves in this way, we cannot begin to assume any real mastery over ourselves. In the final analysis, self-mastery and self-control set the stage for our emergence as wholesome, productive human beings—as *entelechies*, to use that wonderful Aristotelian term. So long as we are influenced by "outside" beings (that is, outside our "I" being, regardless of whether they operate in our other bodies), we are not truly free. Thus the abused child defense, the "Twinkie" defense, and the insanity plea all tend to excuse or promote irresponsible behavior. And there seems to be a growing number of lawyers and psychotherapists bent on promoting such self-indulgences, with hardly a thought for the terrible social consequences of what they advocate. On the other hand, psychiatrists such as William Glasser have found great efficacy in teaching their patients to assume increasing responsibility for their behavior. Glasser's seminal work *Reality Therapy: A New Approach to Psychiatry* is highly recommended in this regard and serves to establish a powerful bridgehead against the torrent of popular, self-indulgent therapies flowing from Freud and his many intellectual and spiritual progeny.

A major difficulty in attempting to write about evil is the painful awareness of the huge amount of relevant material that, because of its complexity, cannot be included in this work. It would simply take us too far from our subject to give here an adequate treatment of Steiner's observations about the prehistory of the earth, for instance (although we will briefly touch on them later) or to present a meaningful treatment of the celestial hierarchy, that vast choir of divine spiritual beings who stand ever ready to assist us in our earnest struggle against evil. Yet all these things and more are necessary if we hope to gain a fuller understanding of evil. To understand the role of evil in our time, it is necessary to know the mission of evil for all time. And to know the mission of evil for all time (and, of course, the good) is to begin to glimpse what it means to be a human being in the fullest sense of the word.

Chapter Four

The Eternal Feminine

(Chorus Mysticus:)
Alles Vergängliche
Ist nur ein Gleichnis;
Das Unzulängliche,
Hier wird's Ereignis;
Das Unbeschreibliche,
Hier ist's getan;
Das Ewig-Weibliche
Zieht uns hinan.

What is destructible
Is but a parable;
What fails ineluctably,
The undeclarable,
Here it was seen,
Here it was action;
The Eternal Feminine
Leads to perfection.
—Goethe, *Faust*, part 2
(Walter Kaufmann translation)

WITH THESE SOLEMN, soul-stirring words, among the most evocative in all of literature, Goethe drops the curtain on his great epic drama, *Faust*, leaving us with a profound mystery: Who, where, is the eternal-feminine?

"All that perishes or passes away is but a semblance; What must fail (evil), here it was shown; What cannot be described, here has been done; The Eternal Feminine leads us upward and on," to use my own crude words. Faust's lengthy bout with the Satan/devil, Mephistopheles, stirs an archetypal chord in all of us. Faust is "everyman" searching for knowledge and wisdom, and he calls on Mephistopheles to assist him. We, too, are on a search for knowledge and wisdom, and we, too, must get to know Mephistopheles (Lucifer and Ahriman) to do it. We can not defeat our enemies by ignoring them or by running away from them. In that way, obviously, they would have already defeated us. On the contrary, we must seek out our adversaries; we must know our enemies, uncover their hiding places, and fight them on our terms. The battle must be and is being fought on our terrain: the human soul.

We cannot know the light unless we also know the dark. Without darkness as its contrast, the entire concept of light would be meaningless. Since we're dealing with two adversaries who generate illusions and deceptions of light and dark, we can be sure that they are not as they may first appear. They are "veiled," for want of a better term. Let's see if we can at least partially unveil one of our enemies to get a better picture of his true nature:

As I was working on the first draft of the last chapter I was reminded that books written today should be in a "gender-universal" style (what used to be called "gender neutral"). Now this is a beautiful ideal, and I certainly don't want to offend anyone with a clumsy, heavy-handed, masculine style. Why, then, did I experience a certain amount of anger when I was reminded of this stylistic need? Not just the style but, more important, the syntax had to be such that some other word had to be substituted for the word *man* when used in accordance with the *Oxford English Dictionary's* first definition of the word: "a human being (irrespective of sex or age)." To find out, I slipped into my holoscopic persona and set about trying to analyze where my anger was coming from. Was it another one of those clever demons silently screaming from the dark recesses of my soul? Or was there, perhaps, some even more sinister source for my anger?

Attempting to write in a gender-universal manner obviously imposes certain limitations on ones style. It also detracts from the artistry of our beautiful English language. ("So God created man/woman in His/Her own image; in the image of God created He/She him/her.") Yet that was not enough. My anger seemed to run a little deeper than from such obvious silliness. It seemed to arise in opposition to the wider phenomenon of "political correctness" itself. Obviously I was not alone in my frustrations with this imposition, as we shall soon see.

Strongly implicit in political correctness is the element of control; do or speak as I say, or as my group says you should, and everything will be okay, and you will be politically correct. We recall from chapter three that any attempts at controlling others is ahrimanic in nature, that it produces demons in our astral bodies, while the forming of generalizations is a luciferic activity. In gender universality we seem to have both. We also have the elements of polarity, of divisiveness. Of such chauvinistic divisiveness you will recall Steiner's words from chapter two about the tendency he sees for this to continue to develop to the point where people become so divisive that they will eventually be at war within themselves. This is the result of various interest groups vying for their own way under Ahriman's inspiration.

One of the wittiest and most convincing articles I've yet seen for a return to sanity in the English language was written by Christy Barnes, late publisher and editor of Adonis Press. She points out in "To Be or Not to Be Human," that we have no trouble distinguishing the word *light* from its cousin *light* as used in the following sentence: "The early morning light turned the leaves golden as they fluttered in a light breeze." Why then, she argues, should we have any trouble with *Man* and *man*, as in "Man is nobler than the animals, but a man like your nephew often behaves like one." She then cites politically correct versions of several well-known phrases, including Alexander Pope's famous: "The proper study of mankind is human." [1]

One of my favorite holoscopic instruments I call the "reverscope." It is an optical device I fit over my eye from time to time to see whether things are as they appear or whether there may be something of their opposite nature in them. I have peered through this useful apparatus at big, friendly companies, many churches, and quite a few branches of science, all with interesting results. In other areas of study—the fields of law, modern popular culture, pharmaceutics, medicine, and politics, for example—only a low-power setting of the instrument is required. Let's see if we can find the right setting on our reverscope to examine that wonderful-sounding term "gender universality."

First, we see that it is a beautiful, diaphanous euphemism. The English language has no gender, except for the occasional reference to one's boat or car in the feminine, e.g., "She sure is a beauty!" Gender is a linguistic term. French has two genders, masculine and feminine; German has three, masculine, feminine, and neuter. In most cases the gender has nothing to do with sex; the popular German words for "wife" or "woman," *das Weib,* and the two most common nouns for "girl" or "young lady," *das Mädchen* and *das Fräulein,* are all neuter. Do we resolve the problem of gender universality in English by referring to a human being as an "it"? No, I don't think this is what advocates of gender universality have in mind.

A euphemism is a polite-sounding word or phrase designed to protect the listener's sensitive ears from what may be considered a harsher reality. Ladies go to the "powder room," for example. We use euphemisms every day when we order "beef" or "pork" instead of "cow's flesh" or "pig meat." So long as we know precisely what we're getting, euphemisms are perfectly acceptable. As holoscopists we learn to look through the various polite phrases to the reality behind them. It's a game of hide-and-seek. When we do this with the beautiful-sounding generality "gender universality," we remove this term from its context and examine it more closely, and we find, hiding behind it, the true prompters of those soaring, lofty-sounding utterances—not only the manipulative Ahriman, but also his opposite, who wants to oversimplify things and paint them with broad generalities: Lucifer.

Just as Ahriman represents the false masculine—all that is cold, dark, manipulative, and power hungry—Lucifer represents the false feminine—sweet-sounding words that cloak reality, the euphemisms, and the pride-filled aloofness found in vague generalities and little verbal niceties that sometimes aren't really intended to be so very nice at all. Thus, from now on—not in any attempts at gender universality, but rather, based on what we have learned—we could refer to Lucifer as feminine, as the she-devil. In fact, one of the ways to help us distinguish between Lucifer and Ahriman is to view men as ahrimanic and women as luciferic. How's that for opening up a can of PC worms? If anyone feels offended by this characterization, I apologize. My intent is only to help us understand the differences between these two beings. I could just as well have said that conservatism is ahrimanic and liberalism is luciferic, or that, regarding the threefold social order, the economic sphere is ahrimanic while the cultural sphere is luciferic. We must be able to overcome any deep-seated prejudices if we are to make any progress in these matters. Hence these characterizations are offered merely as seed thoughts. If you feel offended or angered by them, you may want to examine the source of that anger before you can expect to make much progress in holoscopy.

In his fascinating pastel study *Licht und Finsternis* ("Light and Darkness"), Steiner depicts a proud Lucifer in the upper left, looking off into the far distant glories of infinite space (see cover image). The beautiful, light-filled yellows and reds of her profile are contrasted with a dark, leathery, sinister-looking Ahriman, portrayed in heavy blues and purples in the lower right, looking up at Lucifer, "sizing her up," as some might say. Ahriman has cold, calculating eyes, as well as a distinct supra-orbital brow-ridge, a masculine feature that is lacking in Lucifer's profile. Subtly, in the weaving texture of the neutral greens between them, a third figure can be discerned. It is the full figure of a human being weaving in the balance between Lucifer and Ahriman. It is important that we see this figure, that we see ourselves, holding and maintaining the balance between these two powerful polarities. Only from this conscious, balanced perspective can we hope to find not the false masculinity of Ahriman nor the flattering femininity of Lucifer, but the *eternal feminine*, the universal principle of true wisdom that "leads to perfection," as Goethe observed.

While we have seen that Lucifer wants to emasculate our language, we should be aware that Ahriman wants to mechanize it. The clever acronyms used these days in the military, science, and in business are of ahrimanic coinage. And speaking of coinage, Steiner once remarked how delighted he was to be in Britain, with its pounds, crowns, shillings, and ha'pence, and so on.... Alas! Those colorful days are gone. People had to think in those days when they bought something, or when they made change. Today Ahriman counts our change for us in his electronic calculating cash registers. How nice; we don't have to think at all. (Please excuse the sarcasm, but I don't know how else to express effectively my feelings about such contraptions.) Yet, how proud I am—though somewhat amazed—that the U.S., possibly one of the most ahrimanic of countries, is still one of the last great hold-outs against the metric system. Feet, pounds, inches, ounces, the Fahrenheit scale; all these still have a bit of the human in them, as well as a potential for artistry, which is totally lacking in the metric system. If I were the bumper-sticker type, I'd have them make mine "Don't give an inch to metric!"

Steiner warns us that the ahrimanic impulses work very strongly in any numerological system based on the number ten.[2] But we don't have to take Steiner's word for this. All we have to do is enter the arena with a bit of sensitivity and awareness. This is also a good way to get a feeling for how Ahriman works. Think, for instance, about some of the folksy expressions that have been handed down to us from times unacquainted with metric: "I love you a bushel and a peck"; "Give him an inch and he'll take a mile"; or "penny wise and pound foolish." One would find it impossible to convert these sayings into metric. All the artistry, all the humanity would be taken out of them, leaving them clinical, dry, and abstract. They would become a mockery of the originals. Sure, the metric system is easier than the old English system, but easier should never be confused with better.

According to modern spiritual research, the influences of Ahriman and Lucifer wax and wane over time. Steiner asks us to observe the increased ahrimanic nature of certain centennial and millennial occasions.

Normally, Lucifer and Ahriman pretty much balance each other out, but during a century that contains a nine in the hundreds position—for example, the "1900s," the previous century—a particularly strong attack by Lucifer and Ahriman, acting in combination, occurs.

> In earlier times, for example, in A.D. 1000, people were obliged to believe what Ahriman and Lucifer bluffed them into believing, because they had not yet within them the true, conscious Christ impulse. But today we have by our own free will to take this Christ impulse into ourselves in order to resist Lucifer and Ahriman. In our time, Lucifer and Ahriman work particularly strongly in those who see fit to call themselves Christians, without having one iota of true Christianity in them.... Additionally, these two inimical beings will "rage against" those who adhere to the true Christian principles of "I am with you always, even to the end of earthly days," those who direct their lives according to the living, still functioning Christ impulse. When the year 2000 comes, confusion and devastation will prevail. And then no single piece of the wood will remain of our building in Dornach. *(Ibid.)*

The building in Dornach, near Basel, Switzerland, the first Goetheanum, was destroyed by arson New Year's Eve, 1922, less than eight years after Steiner's prediction of its destruction. During its ten years of construction, teams of dedicated individuals from seventeen countries were engaged in carving its huge wooden columns, capitals, and sculptured forms. Its thick, solid, colored glass windows displayed a unique feature developed by Steiner; that of grinding away its various figures and scenes of the spiritual world in such a way that the figures appeared luminous against the darker backgrounds of their individually colored panes.[3]

Some say a crazed cleric was seen near the scene of the fire; others ascribe it to the work of the Nazis. The building has since been replaced with the second Goetheanum, the first architecturally significant structure constructed of reinforced concrete, and of a very different design from the first. In this second building, as well as in that of the first Goetheanum, Steiner avoided the use of right angles wherever possible, since they, like the metric system, provide a dwelling place for the ahrimanic forces. Another bumper sticker might cryptically read, "The right angle is wrong!" It is, however, necessary at floor level, beneath our feet, where ahrimanic demons belong.

A few words about the Nazis are called for here. When Hitler rose to power, he outlawed Steiner's anthroposophy and closed down the Waldorf schools, which had been using Steiner's pedagogical techniques. Anthroposophy itself is never taught to the children in Waldorf schools; nevertheless, because Waldorf encourages children to think for themselves in an independent, artistic manner, Hitler saw this new form of education as a threat to his plan for world domination through racial hatred. Hitler was Steiner's nemesis. Where does he fit into our picture of evil? I wish I could answer this question with more authority, but I will relate here what little I know and let you draw your own conclusion. Hitler could almost be seen as the antipode of everything Steiner stood for. Although twenty-eight years younger than Steiner, Hitler's struggles for power were evidently on Steiner's mind. In 1923 Steiner spoke of him: "If this man rises to power, I can never again work in Germany."[4]

I have it on good, though unconfirmed, authority from a gentleman I met in Scotland around 1980, that his sister had been Hitler's private librarian, and that Hitler's library was well stocked with Steiner's works. I relate this information in the interest of truth, knowing full well that certain demonic powers may use it in a malicious attempt to attack Steiner and his anthroposophy. Nevertheless, truth (if the story is true) has a way of always winning out in the end. Hitler's brutal racist policies, as well as his appeals to a frenzied chauvinism, were clearly antithetical to Steiner's patient, calm, and persevering call for a deeper understanding of the Christ through modern spiritual scientific means.

It seems possible to some that World War II could have been averted if enough people had taken the time and effort during Steiner's time to grasp the basic principles of anthroposophy or, at least, of the fundamentally important concepts of his threefold social order. But Steiner, always mindful of the freedom and dignity of each human being, never used persuasive techniques or propaganda to further his cause. After the war, many people in Germany were heard to say, "Well, I didn't know what was going on; you can't blame me [for the concentration camps, the genocide and mass slaughters, and so on]." But we must remember that there are sins of omission as well as those of commission. Also, we must not forget that in the Germany of 1939, a scant fourteen years after Steiner's death, it was "politically correct" to be a member of the Nazi Party. This political correctness had an insidious side, because it allowed so many people, both members and nonmembers of the Nazi party, to go about the gruesome tasks of murder and torture in the concentration camps during the day, and then go home to a loving family in the evenings with a completely clear conscience. It's been called "the banality of evil" by some who interviewed those people after the war. Perfectly normal people leading perfectly normal family lives, yet capable of committing the most heinous acts of evil. Such is the power of political correctness gone awry and why it is one of our targets earlier in this chapter.

A balanced and well researched perspective of those times can be found in John Cornwell's *Hitler's Pope: The Secret History of Pius XII* (Penguin, 2000). Cornwell shows how Pacelli, as both Secretary of State for the Vatican and later as Pius XII—perhaps because of his strong fixation on an agenda of establishing and preserving the authority of the Holy See in such matters as the selection of Bishops and the control of the schools—somehow lost his perspective on what was happening out in the fields of human endeavor. The result of this oversight was that he played, perhaps unwittingly, into the hands of Hitler. This work, by the way, also provides a unique perspective on the fascinating history of World War II.

Today, the dangers are even greater than in Hitler's time. We are faced with adversaries of enormous power, yet we need have no fear of them if we but waken to the call. Our weapons are at hand, and they are indefeasible; they consist of knowledge of the reality of the spiritual worlds, and the capacity to work together with enthusiasm and good will in the face of an ever-increasing power-grab by the current US Administration. Faith may be shaken, but knowledge remains firm, which is why we are implored to put everything to the test and wake up to current events. Time is extremely short. On September 28, Michaelmas Eve, of 2006, just as this book was going to press, the Senate passed a bill giving the President awesome, unprecedented powers to declare someone an "enemy combatant" and then, without a trial or any protection from the fundamental right of Habeas Corpus, incarcerate that individual for life. Hitler would have loved to have had such a cooperative body of lawmakers.

Just as Goethe leaves us pondering the profound question of the eternal feminine in the closing words of his life-long work, *Faust*, the Bible in its final book, *The Revelation of St John*, leaves us with an equally profound image: the Woman clothed with the sun. Could there be a connection?

The Apocalypse is a deeply occult work. Today's simplistic and frequent admonition in certain circles to avoid the occult is tantamount to saying, "Don't read the Bible; I'll tell you what to think." The holoscopist immediately recognizes the luciferic/ahrimanic character of such words and immediately looks elsewhere for advice. Such an admonition is luciferic in its overly broad generalization and ahrimanic in its attempt to manipulate us; Lucifer and Ahriman working together again as a team. One way to look at it is to view Ahriman as Lucifer's "shadow." Another insight can be gained through a study of projective geometry, particularly as researched by such authors as George Adams, Olive Wicher, H. Keller-von Asten, and others (see bibliography). In this way, Ahriman can be seen as the "pole," or antipode, of Lucifer. After all, there are good and bad scientists and good and bad preachers as well as good and bad areas of the occult. To separate any of them with too strong a wind is to blow away the good wheat with the useless chaff.

Steiner calls Ahriman a "karmic necessity" of Lucifer. One could also see the latter as the "lord of birth" and the former as the "lord of death." The archetypal midwife and the archetypal undertaker might be another way of putting it. But, just as midwives and undertakers are productive, useful, even necessary members of our society, so, too, are Lucifer and Ahriman in their proper place.

It was Eve, a woman, who acted as Lucifer's surrogate in assisting at our birth into the physical realms, and it will be Adam, or Adam Kadmon, who shows the way back to the cosmos. Steiner likens him to Ymir, the giant of Norse mythology, spread out in the cosmos. This great macrocosmic man, or creator, represents externally what the human being is inwardly. A profound truth, Steiner says, lies at the basis of such representations, coming to light more or less imperfectly, depending on the clairvoyant capacities of the various peoples. We find it in the esoteric knowledge of the ancient Hebrews, which lays the foundation for the wisdom of the Old Testament. In Adam Kadmon of the Kabbalah, the macrocosmic man is spread out in the cosmos and, the spiritual investigator advises us, we should form the right concepts of him.

The archetypal, *macrocosmic man*. I am not a Hebrew scholar, so I can't elaborate on the hidden meaning of the words *Adam Kadmon* in that sacred language, but I'm sure this archetypal man has nothing to do with the false masculine promptings of Ahriman. When we see man in this false ahrimanic light, we are tempted to flee into the waiting arms of Lucifer who whispers to us warm, self-satisfying, and diabolical phrases such as "gender universality." The *Oxford English Dictionary* devotes several pages to the word "man," nevertheless, as mentioned, its first definition is "a human being (irrespective of sex or age)." Those who think they have made a step toward resolving the painfully complex problem of women's rights by insisting on "gender universality," or whatever euphemism they may choose, risk soaring into a Luciferic dream on the one hand, and destroying the beauty, artistry, and wisdom of our beloved English tongue on the other. Writers of both sexes might take note of this, because we're faced today with a veritable avalanche of such well-intentioned euphemisms; as we are, on the other hand, with so many impersonal acronyms and mechanistic abbreviations.

This short digression was necessary, because in our quest for the eternal feminine we must make a nodding acquaintance, at the very least, with the false feminine and masculine, Lucifer and Ahriman, as well as with the eternal archetypal masculine, whom we have learned to call Adam Kadmon.

In our search for the eternal feminine, who promises to assist in our joust with evil, we need a common perspective. Let's establish our vantage point where we live, part way up the great vertical polarity of evil, just above the 'good' middle point. We should be a little higher than center, because we need just enough of Lucifer's enthusiasm to warm and loosen Ahriman's frigid, ossifying influence. I would suggest somewhere between three-fifths and two-thirds of the way up. That's where we'll dig in and make our camp, hopefully some day to become a great city.

We will continue our pursuit of the eternal feminine with a useful quotation from the Rev. Emil Bock's work, *The Apocalypse of St John:*

> What, then, can the drama in the twelfth and thirteenth chapters of the Apocalypse teach us who live in the midst of the spiritual conflict of the present age? We must enter into the role of the woman who goes into the wilderness. In the wilderness of solitude and reflection, the help of Michael will be granted us. The wings of the Eagle will be given us. It is not without reason that the Eagle is the sign of John, the evangelist and seer. The eagle wings of the apocalyptic vision carry us to high watch towers, from which we obtain a comprehensive view of our age and a knowledge of the spiritual aspect of world events. Thus we are enabled to triumph over Lucifer's soul realm without spirit, and Ahriman's spirituality without soul. We can aspire to a spirit-filled soul and an ensouled spirituality and can attain to inward sovereignty in both directions. This is the religion of tranquility in the golden mean, the sphere of Christ. It is, at the same time, the sphere of Michael. Although it appears paradoxical, to cultivate tranquility is the most effective way of combating evil. We must not always be aggressive when we fight the spiritual battle. Out of a soul filled with peace a new morality is born.

On Christmas Eve of 1920, as part of a short series of lectures to members of the Anthroposophical Society in Dornach, Switzerland, Rudolf Steiner evoked a mighty, imaginative picture of the need for a revitalized Christmas Festival.[5] In place of the exchanging of gifts and Christmas cards with their usual trite phrases, acts done these days mostly out of habit, he called for a completely new understanding of Christ. We need to find the wisdom that gives birth to love, the Sophia/Maria that gave birth to Jesus; the eternal-feminine that leads us upward and on. We do this by uniting in spirit with the simple shepherds who, through their purity of heart, were allowed to participate in this great event, and also by working to unite with the three Magi, the Wise Men, who, because they were initiates, were also guided to this momentous incursion into the course of human destiny.[6] Both streams can come together in each of us. And both are needed; the purity of love as well as the surety of wisdom, in order to prepare ourselves to be able to participate, to witness, this birth. The choice is ours.

If we choose, as the freest choice we can make, at whatever level of human evolution we may find ourselves, to undergo this *metanoin*, this complete change of the constitution of our souls, then we may be allowed, through divine grace, to stand in the presence of the eternal-feminine, the divine Sophia/Maria.

We are free to choose the direction that our lives will take. Only we, however, can make that choice. This is part of what it means to be human, to be truly human. We are not, we cannot be, constrained to pursue one course or another, either to drift along with the crowd into a void of oblivion or, by our own efforts, to begin the long and arduous ascent to a meaningful apprehension of the spirit, to the wisdom of the spirit, the eternal-feminine.

We have now progressed in our studies to a point where we can revisit the so-called problem of evil as discussed in our introduction. It is the first of three great "cleavers," or wedges, which have been thrust between science and religion, between knowledge and faith. You will recall the three premises of the problem: God is omnipotent, or all-powerful; God is omnibeneficent, or perfectly good; and third, evil exists. Is it possible to resolve this problem without denying any of its three premises? No.

The problem is incapable of solution, because it is improperly worded and is incomplete. It totally ignores the most important element, without which the problem could not be posed in the first place; it ignores the human being who poses such a problem in the first place.

Once we factor in the human being who has the courage or perhaps the bravado to ask such a question, the answer becomes obvious: God is omnipotent, or all-powerful; God is omnibeneficent, or all-good; and evil exists *so that human beings can become free*. It is impossible to postulate a free human being who is unable to commit evil. If there were no possibility to commit evil, we would be constrained to do only the good, and hence we would not have the possibility of complete freedom. In addition to laying the foundation for our future freedom, evil strengthens us immensely. Or, as Steiner puts it: "The wise guidance of the world allowed humans to become evil and gave us the possibility of doing harm, so that in repairing the harm and overcoming the evil we can become stronger in the course of karmic development than we would have become had we reached our goal without effort. This is how we should understand the significance and justification of obstacles and hindrances." [7]

What greater act of love could there be than to create a race of human beings, and then allow those humans to choose their own destiny? And what greater words could be chosen to depict this free choice than to give them the opportunity "to eat of the Tree of Knowledge of Good and Evil?" In the final analysis, we could never become free if we didn't have at least the potential to commit evil. This becomes self-evident after only a few moments of unbiased reflection. But there is a greater act of love than the act of creating beings who have the capacity for freedom; it is the willingness to suffer and die for those you have created, to put yourself utterly at their mercy, and still leave them free.

The full impact and importance of Christ's supreme act of love, his willingness to suffer by bowing to the evil machinations within each of us, so that we, of our own free will, might decide whether to follow him, can scarcely be grasped by human intelligence. Our intelligence must be raised to this task, however, and to the task of discerning in the external phenomena the forces and beings that interpenetrate our spiritual space. Many of the ills in our society today that seem only natural will be explained only when we begin to see and understand the disturbing, retarding forces we're really dealing with. One who has insight, however, may be in a position to help keep others free from the disturbing influences of these beings. As spiritual investigation tells us,

> You will experience all sorts of crass cultural phenomena in the near future. You will find that those standing within them will look upon those people as dreamers who call things by their right names. The world has reached the stage where those who know reality are called dreamers and visionaries, whereas the real ones caught in dreams are those who wish to cling only to the external. The progress of civilization rests upon people's penetrating with knowledge into the character of the hostile powers. Knowledge, when understood in the sense often expressed here, is something that will, from the anthroposophical spiritual stream, bring a certain saying to true realization. It is the saying that we have learned in Christian esotericism, and that the leader of Christian life proclaimed to his followers: "Ye shall know the truth and the truth shall make you free." Knowledge of full and complete truth and reality can make humans free, and wholly and entirely human.[8]

This is not a "post-Christian" age, as many would have us believe; it is a *pre*-Christian age. In many respects we are still pagans, barely able to hear that still, small voice of the one crying in the wilderness, the wilderness of our souls. Our task in the course of this work is to harken to that voice and to examine the remaining two devastating cleavers that have been thrust between the two great camps of science and religion. Only when these two camps are reunited in truth, harmony, and good will can we hope to achieve success in our struggle with evil.

CHAPTER FIVE

REPENTANCE, THE ULTIMATE PARADIGM SHIFT

(Repent!—the changing of one's consciousness.
Or, to use the scientific term: to undergo a paradigm shift.)

"Change the constitution of your soul! (*Metanoiete*)
for the kingdom of heaven is near."
—JOHN THE BAPTIST, Matthew 3:2
—JESUS CHRIST, Matthew 4:17

So far, we have covered a vast amount of territory. For many it will be new, uncharted land, unfamiliar and a bit strange. We were introduced to the concept of "holoscopy," along with a few of its tools, including reverence for truth—not, please note, for a particular human being, but for *truth*. We were also introduced to the "reverscope," together with a few of its more obvious applications, for example the ability to see in many institutions of human endeavor strong elements of the opposite of what an institution purports to represent. We will continue working with this powerful instrument of observation, but now we will adjust it to its maximum setting and see what wonders await.

To do this effectively, we need to lift ourselves "by our own bootstraps" to a mode of consciousness that transcends our everyday level of subjugation to characterological predispositions, prejudices, and the sway of semi-hidden sympathies and antipathies, or the prevailing pressures of public opinion. Some will find this an easier task than others, but it is helpful to know that our efforts, however feeble and seemingly ineffective at first, are met by corresponding efforts "from the other side" to help us. Then, as we persevere in our attempts to surmount the canyons of habit and the thickets of confusion, we become increasingly aware of the presence of a lifeline, for want of a better term, being offered to assist us in our clambering. Such a lifeline must be thoroughly tested before we can trust our future ascent to its integrity. How can we know that such a lifeline exists? The answer is as simple as it is difficult: You cannot know until you make the effort to know. For many years, astronomers had to retire to a laboratory to grind and polish the lenses and mirrors of their telescopes; similarly, holoscopists retire to a laboratory to grind, polish, and fine-tune the instruments of perception they will need in their quest for enlightenment. There are no store-bought holoscopes.

Nor can we let the mocking winds of a perfidious public opinion steer us off our course. "I am the master of my fate; I am the captain of my soul," wrote William Ernest Henley more than a hundred years ago. His "Invictus" stirs our souls to this day, even though all he could see "beyond this place of wrath and tears" was the looming horror of the shade.[1]

Courage is another of the many tools holoscopy offers us, courage that can come only from knowledge of what lies in that shade or unseen region. Blind faith no longer suffices for those with intellectual integrity. Yet this is courage fired with enthusiasm, as discussed earlier, enthusiasm borne by the capacity to see, within even the most horrific and despicable of evil deeds, a higher good that allows such evil to seemingly prevail. As Aurobindo puts it: "Oh blessed be thee, misfortune, for through thee I have seen the face of my beloved."[2] Aurobindo's *lover* has nothing to do with the popular concept of that term. It is rather a divine revelation, a personal encounter he was able to work his way toward, a higher reality and level of perception than ordinary consciousness permits. He recognizes that only through overcoming his misfortunes was he able to do this.

Now that we have met our two enemy/friends, or friendly enemies if you prefer, Lucifer and Ahriman, who provide us with these misfortunes in such abundance, it is necessary for us to start overcoming them and look for a true friend, our true lover. We have seen how Lucifer and Ahriman, while working on a macrocosmic scale—that is, in world events—also work on a microcosmic scale within each of us. And we've seen that we must become aware of their inner promptings if we are to have any hope of striking a balance between their opposing, inimical powers. We have seen, too (in chapter 3), how phantoms are produced in the physical body with every lie we utter, even those fabricated for a supposedly good cause. We have also seen how, through bad laws and unjust social measures, specters are generated in our etheric bodies. And, finally, we've seen that, whenever we attempt to control the free will of others by working on their souls in an unjust, manipulative manner, we generate demons in our astral bodies.

We have also seen how materialists reject such invisible entities as unworthy of consideration. But the holoscopist, rather than dismissing any possibility of their existence without further examination, places these new-found concepts on what we could call one's "raised-eyebrow shelf." We are skeptical when we first encounter such seemingly ridiculous notions. The "raised-eyebrow shelf" is not a mental garbage can, but more like the new acquisitions section of a museum; it is visited frequently and enthusiastically. The artifacts in this section are examined, tested, and pored over until, perhaps years later, they may be finally cataloged and added to that part of our mental construct we call "knowledge," or relegated to the basement storage area. After all, museums would be awfully boring if they contained the same old stones and bones and relics every time we visited. Why then, in that marvelous museum of the mind, do so many curators dismiss out-of-hand any new acquisitions that do not merely augment, in some small way, their existing and previously cataloged collections? More than willing, the holoscopic curator is eager to find new evidence, especially if it adds to one's scientific collection and compels a re-cataloging of the vast areas of previously acquired treasures.

Pressing the metaphor just a bit further, let's assume that, among the experts we hire to help oversee the enlargement of our museum, one prevents us from testing the artifacts in his department. He is the sole authority, and his word alone should suffice, at least in his opinion, in sorting and cataloging all the new acquisitions that come under his purview. Further, he makes no allowance for calling in other experts to test and verify his findings.

Such is the condition we encounter when we pursue many of the ancient paths of enlightenment, paths intended for an earlier condition of consciousness, before we had the power of analytical thinking at our disposal. In those days, before the Renaissance, we were asked to place ourselves in subservience to an outside authority, to a guru, an expert who told us what to do, what to think and how to feel if we were to have any success in our quest for enlightenment. Such practices were absolutely appropriate in previous ages when we had a more childlike consciousness; but they run counter to one of the main themes of this work and to the true spirit of scientific inquiry—that is to say, that we, you, become the expert. This is not in any way to denigrate the devoted practices of those who choose to follow such paths. There is a great richness in the heritage of the past. In a path of development for modern Western thinkers, however, there is a healthy repugnance toward blindly following teachers who takes it upon themselves to oversee, with unquestioned authority, the development of our soul-spiritual life. After all, anyone who has followed the meteoric course of some popular Eastern spiritual teachers during the past forty years know that there are both good and bad gurus. Many of those "meteors" have ended their careers as pitiful cinders or mere embers of their former glory, their false lights occluded by the never-ending search for the illumination of real truth and, in some cases, having succumbed to today's wide-spread and powerful temptations, particularly in the West—temptations of alcohol and other substance abuse, as well as puffery, self-aggrandizement, and the power to control others.

The great lure of exotic Eastern occult teachings has captivated Western seekers for generations. Wondrous tales of advanced Eastern masters and gurus who perform all kinds of miracles and feats of magic quite naturally have their appeal. Who can blame idealistic aspirants for traveling half-way around the globe in their search for enlightenment? Little do they suspect that they incarnated here in the West because right here, right under their noses, is the most demanding, most rewarding path of all—spiritual science: a path that can be verified and tested every step of the way.

Returning to our mental museum, what's a curator to do? We certainly cannot pretend to have anything like a complete museum without at least a hall of Eastern wisdom. I suggest we open such a hall, gurus and all, and that we visit it occasionally for the priceless wisdom we can garner there. I also suggest, however, that we not accept the authority of any gurus without first putting them to the same standards of verification we would apply to any other teacher or teaching. This also applies, alas, to our beloved Sri Aurobindo, who, in part one of his *Letters on Yoga*, propounds a very compelling argument as to why the guru's authority should not be questioned.[3] My reply to him would be that the problem lies not in the questioning but in how carefully the questions are crafted. It is true that one can easily get lost in an endless chain of questions, as he says—an infinite regress, stemming from idle curiosity. In the Western tradition, St. Augustine, too, was aware of this danger, and he dealt with it in a way similar to that of Aurobindo. Later, we will give an example of the folly of such inquiry and endless questioning (as well as its fruits, when not taken too far) when we discuss the interesting example of a hayloft in a carriage house. When a carefully considered question arises and, after perhaps years of pondering and meditation, still yields to no meaningful answer, it would not only be appropriate but also necessary for it to be asked. Nonetheless, sincere study, sometimes in seemingly unrelated fields, will sometimes yield the answer we are seeking, especially if we ponder the new material with enough diligence. The Gospels in particular, along with much of the New Testament, are quite fruitful in this regard, but they must be read and understood in a somewhat unorthodox way—one based on spiritual scientific investigation and knowledge, not solely on tradition or conventional scholarship and authority, which frequently leads to nothing but rancor and dispute.

At this point, therefore, the wise holoscopist places Sri Aurobindo, along with his priceless wisdom, in the newly-created Hall of Eastern Wisdom. He is one of our most prized and valued exhibits, but certainly not our guru. Neither science nor religion can arrogate to themselves such a position of unquestioned authority. Appeals to the certitude of calculation, on the one hand, or to a warm, fuzzy emotional "high," on the other, merely impede our search for a higher truth. It's no longer a question of embracing science or religion in a blind, intellectually lazy way. Certainly we can see that both science and religion offer priceless gifts of knowledge, thus they are both included in the holoscopist's museum. It is this latter hall, the Hall of Religion, to which we now turn.

At this point I must ask the reader's indulgence. When I attempt to write about the Christ, I am overcome with an awesome sense of inadequacy and incompetence. Yet, write about him I must, because no treatment of this vast subject of evil could possibly be presented in a balanced way without at least a hint of the great powers for the good that operate behind the scenes of this mighty drama. What follows should be seen as only a hint and the briefest of introductions to this vast subject. It is inspired by Rudolf Steiner, that great Christian initiate who spoke and wrote about what he could see and verify in the spiritual worlds. After more than thirty-five years of rigorous testing I, too, have been able to verify some of his observations on these matters.

Much of Steiner's teachings about Christ can be verified by anyone willing to make the effort to develop a healthy, human understanding and an open attitude of good will. One cannot simply learn the facts by rote and then reproduce them, unembellished, as one might on a final exam in chemistry or physics. That would be a travesty, a mocking caricature of any true and serious teaching. No one can convince anyone else of the truth, beauty, or goodness of Steiner's teachings without the willingness to bring the teachings repeatedly and regularly before the soul's light of consciousness. One must challenge them, not from a field of prejudice or foregone conclusions, but in the manner of a knight errant in search of the greatest mystery of the world—the quest for the Holy Grail—wielding in one hand the sword of truth, cutting away all falsehood, and in the other a shield of healthy skepticism. I am well aware of my words' inadequacy as I attempt to convey the following material. I ask only that any faults found here be placed where they belong—at my feet, not at those of Dr. Steiner.

The Bible tells us that the Spirit of God descended into the body of Jesus of Nazareth while he was being baptized by John in the Jordan. Spiritual investigation confirms that this momentous event was the actual incarnation of Christ into the specially prepared human body of Jesus. This baptism begins the three-and-a-half year sojourn of Christ on the plane of physical consciousness and activity. But we can't simply accept such events on someone else's authority, a practice we have already seen as inconsistent with healthy human understanding. Can we, then, accept them simply because they are recorded in the Gospels? With this question, we face the second great cleaver that, since about the fifteenth century, has gouged a vast chasm between science and religion, between knowledge and faith. You will recall that the first cleaver was what philosophers and theologians call "the problem of evil," which we touched on in the introduction and in chapter 4. The theodicy (a term used for the various attempts to resolve the problem of evil) we proposed then was that evil exists so that people can become free.

We'll call this second cleaver the "cleaver of incredulity." In the simplest terms, it has to do with the suspicions of many scientists, and the lack of credibility they ascribe to many religious views. As a defense and consequence of this, many in the religious camp view certain scientific theories with equal suspicion. Can this second problem be resolved? Is there a mode of serious inquiry into spiritual matters such that it could be called "scientific"? And can the results of such spiritual investigation be so meaningful and nourishing to the human soul that even the most ardent advocate of "blind faith" might find them acceptable? The main premise of this entire work is that the answers to these two important questions are in the affirmative. It is a qualified affirmation, however, because there are no *prima facie* answers to them; one has to dig for a meaningful solution. This book is addressed to such "diggers." Another qualification lies in the obvious ardor in both camps. From the so-called creationists, on the one hand, to the "evolutionists" on the other, the battle has been clearly joined for many years. One camp cloaks itself in a dogmatic interpretation of the Bible, and the other in an equally dogmatic interpretation of Darwin, Newton, and Kant. One camp calls upon the luciferic pride of a holy certitude, while the other dwells in the ahrimanic arrogance of "scientific" proof and technical prowess. Christians are supposed to be humble people, and scientists are supposed to be open-minded. Nevertheless, it's easy to see that the more people embrace either camp with ardor, heat, and passion, the less are they what they purport to be. This polarization can never be resolved by either side so long as strident "pro-lifers" (a clever euphemism for anti-abortionists) think they can advance their cause by killing abortion doctors, which is an extreme example of "anti-life." Nor can it be won while skeptical scientists, however noble their rationale, refuse to look at all the pertinent data—or worse, attempt to manipulate scientific tests or interpretations to advance their position. Further, it becomes obvious to even the casual observer that, by stridently upholding one pole of a dispute, the other pole is almost automatically strengthened.

Now, before I am banned in the Bible Belt, I'd better explain what I mean by my reference to anti-abortionists killing abortion doctors. Consider: If I climb to a pulpit or shout through a megaphone at some rally and advocate hatred and vituperation against the "pro-choice" people, calling them murderers and child killers or whatever, then I have to accept some of the responsibility if, even years later, some unstable individual decides to shoot one of those doctors. In a way, I'm even more responsible, because I initiated the hatred that resulted, ultimately, in a person's death. Freedom demands the acceptance of responsibility for our actions and our thoughts. There can be no freedom without its necessary corollary: responsibility.

One more example should be mentioned before we return to the critically important battle between science and religion. If I deposit money in a bank, which then invests my funds in the construction of, say, a brewery or a distillery, I become karmically involved with that enterprise. My money is going into building that brewery. No matter what the bank decides to do with the money, it's still mine, and I am karmically responsible for its use. As more people become aware of this hidden aspect of karma, they naturally seek more responsible vehicles for their investments. One such vehicle is the New Century Bank, where investors can determine which causes their money will be applied to.[4]

In his justifiably popular *Small is Beautiful: Economics as if People Mattered*, Fritz Schumacher places the battle right where it belongs: "We have become confused as to what our convictions really are. The great ideas of the nineteenth century may fill our minds in one way or another, but our hearts do not believe in them all the same. Mind and heart are at war with one another, not, as is commonly asserted, reason and faith."[5] In the final analysis, it is in our hearts that this battle is taking place, for what good can we do to agitate for a union of science and religion while our heads are battling to overcome our hearts? Writ large and laid out in society as a whole, this battle in our souls can be seen as the seemingly intractable and endless dispute between science and religion.

Let's take a closer look at both these camps and see if we can garner more insight into this age-old dispute. First, the fundamentalists of the Christian persuasion.

The Gospels were written at a time when the luciferic wisdom permeated the cultures of both East and West far more than it does today. Therefore, during the early centuries of Christianity, people read them and understood them in a way different from today's more scientific, analytical way of thinking. Consciousness changes as humanity evolves. An indisputable testimonial to this fact can be seen in the pyramids of Egypt, for example—those mute, powerful, enigmatic temples of initiation whose construction techniques today's analytical consciousness cannot even fathom, let alone duplicate.

As human consciousness changes through the eons, so must the mode of teaching. The great initiates of the past simply wouldn't have been understood if they had attempted to portray the eternal verities to the ancient Egyptians or Hebrews in the spiritual scientific way appropriate for today's consciousness. Nor would they be understood by us today if they used the methods of instruction of those times. Even two thousand years ago, during Greco-Roman times, the mode of teaching had to be different. The Gospels cannot be analyzed in the way we analyze a specimen of DNA. They need to be explained to us by someone who can "see" and verify what has been seen in the infinite spiritual realms. Anyone who is bilingual will attest to the difficulties of translating even a modest line of poetry, let alone a deeply significant religious passage. Add to this the radical shift in consciousness from one era to another two thousand years later, and the difficulties become even more apparent. Today we need a science of the spirit. There is far too much pretense in these matters. Many people merely pretend to understand the Gospels, strutting about on a stage as they sometimes do, before their eager flock and a bank of television cameras, stirring up in some cases all kinds of sacrosanct mischief and self-righteous wrongdoings. There is no choice. Today we need a new science, a science of the spirit that can be verified and tested like any other science.

Saul's "vision" at the gate of Damascus, for example, was far more than that; it was a holy initiation by Christ Himself, not a hallucination as some sceptics claim. This experience transformed him totally and as a result, as Paul, he was able to spread Christianity more effectively than any other person of his time. Such is the profound nature of a true Christian initiation.

A deeper understanding of the Gospels in the light of spiritual science is the only way such truths can be unveiled. Then the profound wisdom behind the words, hidden from even the most gifted scholars, can come to light in human consciousness. The Gospels are written from four, seemingly contradictory perspectives; this serves as a protection from excessively literal interpretations. In spite of this protection, many sects persist in single-minded approaches that lead to gross distortions.

The result is stupefaction and hallucination—a perfect playground for Ahriman. As Steiner puts it, "In the absolute sense, nothing is good in itself, but is always good or bad according to the use to which it is put. The best can be the worst if wrongly used. Sublime though they are, the Gospels can also have the opposite effect if people are too lazy to search for a deeper understanding based on spiritual science."[6]

To really understand the Gospel of John, it is absolutely essential to understand, for example, the mystery behind the raising of Lazarus. Scholars have no hope of understanding this mighty Gospel without this important key, which is provided only by science of the spirit.[7] This same key, by the way, also helps us understand the significance of John's Revelation. Without initiation science, we can only guess at its true significance and hidden meanings.

Not only theologians but scientists, too, have their "gospels." Some, especially those few who see today's science as the only way to look at reality, can be just as dogmatic as their clerical brethren.

To protect the innocent, we'll use a hypothetical example. Some years ago I bought a beautiful old Victorian home with a large carriage house at the rear of the property. Naturally, the house was our primary concern, so we didn't really analyze the condition of the carriage house as well as we should have before buying the place. Upkeep had become a financial burden for the previous owner who had spent most of her time and money caring for her aged mother, so there were a number of jobs that needed to be done about the place. One problem area was the carriage house. Two large colonies of voracious carpenter ants had invaded the floor of the hayloft above the garage area and had made two large portions of its floor unsafe. Additionally, dry rot had attacked the same two areas.

Here's where the story gets hypothetical. Imagine me setting out to discover the cause of the diseased floor in the manner of the most respected science of our day. How would I go about this study? Well, first I'd probably call in the specialists. The floor is rotten, so I'd bring in experts on wood rot. Assuming I had the money for this hypothetical experiment, I'd also hire an entomologist to determine what type of ant was responsible for the destruction and how that particular species could best be eradicated. These learned doctors would get down on their knees and perhaps microscopically examine the hayloft floor. The former would probably prescribe some kind of a wood preservative, while the latter might explain, "Aha, *Formica pennsylvanica,* a notorious species of carpenter ant," and would then prescribe a poisonous substance to eradicate the offending creatures. Both individuals would have been correct in their diagnoses and in their treatment; one cannot argue with that. Not that any great scientific breakthroughs would have been accomplished, but the point is that both would have been correct. As far as solving the problem, however, they would have been wrong.

Leaving these gentlemen on their knees in the hayloft for the moment (an uncharacteristic gesture for most scientists today), let's ask how a holoscopist might look at the problem. One would spend some time carefully inspecting the entire barn, and then perhaps ask a few questions about the previous owner. Finally, one would make a diagnosis: "The problem is not the carpenter ants or the dry rot. The problem is the poor landlady who formerly owned the place." Well, back in those days I didn't know anything about holoscopy, so I probably would have thought such an approach was a little daft. Nevertheless, let's assume I would have had the courtesy to ask the meaning of such a remark. "Do you see the roof on both sides of the hay door gable? The flashing is gone, and the roof has been leaking for years. That's why there were two areas of infestation, each directly under the missing flashings. The former landlady, if she had the money and the interest in the place, would have kept the roof in better repair. Until your roof is repaired you cannot solve the problem of the floor beneath it."

This little example also illustrates questions of idle curiosity and the endless chain of causality (which we already discussed briefly in this chapter), such as: Why was she poor? Why didn't she take more interest in the place? Why was her mother ill? But such regresses would lead us too far from the nexus of our immediate concern: the damaged floor of the hayloft. Holoscopy calls for a balanced approach to such inquiry, as well as an examination of the plurality of causation.

Another hypothetical: A little boy is inflating a large red balloon. On his balloon are schools of tiny, microscopic scientists busily engaged in seeking answers to some of the enigmatic questions posed by the strange nature of their rubbery universe. Using the best and most up-to-date instruments of their world, they discover that the spaces between the molecules of the balloon are expanding. Their observations up to this point have been correct. Then they do a bit of reverse extrapolation and hypothesize about a time when there was no space between the molecules, yielding an interesting theory about the origin of their ballooning universe. With time, the theory assumes the accretions of fact, though they still refer to it as a theory. They call it "the big-bang theory" of the origin of their universe. At this point the little boy picks up a tiny, portentous pin...

So much for the highly touted purely reductionist approach to thinking. Pure reductionism is erroneous. It is false thinking, because, as we have seen, it is incomplete. We have witnessed two examples of prima facie evidence showing clearly its awesome shortcomings. However, when used holoscopically, it becomes just one of many ways to examine a problem and it can be very useful as a temporary mode of thought.

Turning now to the less hypothetical, we can use these examples to see more clearly, if at first only by analogy, some limitations of natural science as it is practiced today. We'll start by using the automobile as an example.

When we buy a vehicle, our primary concern is transportation. Each time we use it, we want to get from point A to point B and back. But what wonderful choices we have; make, model, style, color, and an almost endless combination of options. Further, we can select a dump truck, an earth mover, an all-terrain vehicle, an RV, SUV, or a pickup, depending on what we plan to carry with us and on the kinds of jobs we have to do. A similar choice occurs before birth, before we incarnate. We have all sorts of styles, colors, and capacities from which to choose. But we must not confuse the vehicle with the driver—the material, temporal body must not be confused with the human being, the driver, who animates and directs the body.

For several decades there has been a worldwide, concerted effort to map human genetic material. Called the Human Genome Project, this multi-billion dollar endeavor has tracked down many thousands of human genes in the hope of discovering how they function in order to determine what makes human beings tick and what genes predispose or cause which diseases. The mapping is only the first phase; the truly daunting challenges will arise from attempts to determine the almost endless permutations and combinations of genetic interactivity. Aside from the formidable array of ethical problems this stirs up (insurance companies, for instance, or prospective employers, may gain access to this genetic information for their policyholders or job applicants), advocates of this project are also hoping to determine what makes one individual different from another. Now I don't want to sound like I'm criticizing the valiant efforts of the thousands of molecular biologists engaged in this project, but isn't this a bit like minutely examining a person's car in order to try to determine whether that individual will be driving to a monastery or to Las Vegas? From the human perspective, the important question is not whether we're driving a Ford or a Chevy; rather, we should ask: Where are we taking that vehicle?

Francis S. Collins, M.D., Ph.D., director of the National Human Genome Research Institute (NHGRI), who oversees the entire Human Genome Project, knows where he's going. As this book was going to press he was seen on Book TV, (C-SPAN 2), talking about his new book, *The Language of God: A Scientist Presents Evidence for Belief* (Free Press, 2006). In a calm, matter-of-fact way, Collins explained how he had been a life-long atheist because he "had never thought about it before." So he decided to think about it. The result was that he became a practicing Christian. I have not had time yet to review his book, but one quote from his talk stood out, "When you do science, you *are* doing religion." My thoughts exactly!

In a gentle and patient manner, author Craig Holdrege also takes us somewhere worth going. In his *Genetics and the Manipulation of Life: The*

Forgotten Factor of Context, he leads us step-by-step through a magical forest and teaches us how to look objectively and dispassionately at nature. We learn to study the various plants in context; we see, perhaps for the first time consciously, how a basswood tree looks when growing on the northern slope of a mountain in Switzerland among other trees in a thick, high forest. He then compares this tall, almost spindly specimen with another of the same species on the dry, southern slope, where it stands alone and is exposed to the elements. Here it becomes a low-growing bush. Starting with this example of contextual, environmental influence, he brings before our mind's eye many other examples of naturally occurring variations. He then enters the modern field of genetic research through its historical roots. Along the way, Holdrege raises some important questions about the basic assumptions that form the foundation of the Human Genome Project. The work ends with a quiet but far-reaching appeal:

> It becomes eminently important, therefore, to examine the way we have chosen, or been taught, to grasp the world. This is the only means of establishing a conscious connection with the effects of our actions. It is the basis for taking responsibility.
>
> A contextual approach is not to be seen as just another solidified doctrine or theory. Rather, it is a necessary complement to the prevailing conceptions and practices of contemporary science. It is a way of making science a healthier whole, modeled after the organisms it studies. (p. 173)

What Holdrege calls a "contextual approach" we are calling a "holoscopic approach." It is precisely the lack of such an approach, or the lack of a reverence for the *whole* truth, that has placed science in the precarious position it finds itself today.

Just how precarious is this reductionist science that refuses to look at the larger picture and the long-range effects of implementing its findings? Well, for starters, some scientists wash their hands of all responsibility, saying, "That's technology, not science. We can't be held accountable for what technology does." Yet, say, if I open a door in mid-winter, and a cold draft blows in, would it be justifiable for me to say, "That's the fault of the cold air, not me. Can I help it if it's cold outside? All I did was open the door." And yet that's precisely the short-sighted attitude some scientists have adopted toward the awful results of the many doors they are opening. What's more, scientists are not only opening doors, they're tearing them down and letting in all sorts of grief. Then they're chopping the doors up and throwing the wood into the wood-stove in a futile effort to keep warm. Once science opens a door, it stays open. It's no wonder that the warning calls from so many critics are beginning to be heard.

One such is David Ehrenfeld who, in "A Techno-Pox Upon the Land," cites several startling accounts of technology gone awry.[8] One is the injection of recombinant Bovine Growth Hormone (rBGH) into cows to make them produce more milk. In addition to its many serious side effects on the animals themselves (including bloating, diarrhea, diseases of the knees and feet, feeding disorders, and fevers), an indirect effect is that they now require more protein in their diets. As a result, ground offal, or "animal by-products," is added to their daily feed. But cows are vegetarians; they are not designed to eat meat and can't handle it. The result? *Bovine spongiform encephalopathy*, or "mad cow disease," and its seemingly related human counterpart, Creutzfeldt-Jakob disease. How far must the short-sighted, reductionistic "I'm not responsible" attitude go before we wake up? Small wonder that science is coming under such critical examination.

Two such critics, whose voices deserve a much wider audience, are Jeremy Rifkin and Pulitzer Prize-winning author Laurie Garrett. Rifkin's *Biotech Century*, while providing a comprehensive survey of all the major advances in the biotech industry up to the end of the last century, also raises serious questions about how these exciting advances can easily go amok. Garrett's work, *The Coming Plague*, strikes an even more somber note. She actually predicts a plague, no ifs, ands, or buts about it. Both books are well researched, well written, and full of appropriate references. Many other such works are readily available, and some of the early ones are considered classics, so we need not cite them here.

Scientists love mysteries, or at least they proclaim they do. For some reason, however, there are certain areas of the mysterious that are "off limits" and seemingly proscribed from all rational scientific investigation. One such area is holism. Jim Lovelock, proponent of the Gaia Hypothesis, says in *Complexity: Life at the Edge of Chaos*: "Biologists have fought long battles against vitalism, animism, anything that smacks of some kind of force beyond the immediate mechanics of the system. So, anything that sounds holistic—a dirty word in itself—is viewed with suspicion. I don't have an instinctive reaction against words like that." To Lovelock's credit he's not afraid to use words that may occasionally dis the doctrinaire members of his once-noble profession.

Another taboo area is homeopathic medicine. Its proscription stems from the dilemma that, if it works (as proven countless times), then the entire materialistic worldview of modern science would be shaken and require reexamination from its very roots. Another probable reason is that homeopathy is very inexpensive, and large allopathic drug houses can see no profit in it. What is this mysterious homeopathy? Briefly, it is the careful selection of a material, often a poison, that produces a specific array of symptoms when administered to volunteers in small allopathic doses. These symptoms are matched with those of the disease or ailment being treated. The material is then diluted (homeopaths call it potentization) with a harmless substance such as lactose in a series of steps that involves "succussion," or extreme agitation. What makes this interesting from a holoscopic perspective (and such an anathema from the materialist's) is that after a certain number of such potentizations Avogadro's law dictates that not one molecule of the original substance remains.[9] Yet something, we'll call it a non-material *essence*, is present in the remedy which mobilizes the body's defenses against the disease. Many insomniacs, for example, have found that taking potentized coffee (Coffea cruda) at bedtime helps promote a good night's sleep.

My purpose in this short disquisition is not to defend homeopathy—there are many who are far more qualified than me to do that—but rather to attack the materialistic and decidedly unscientific attitude of all those who, disguised as scientists, condemn it *a priori* with no attempts at objective evaluation. As a holoscopist I have a great love for the sciences, but only insofar as they preserve a vital reverence for truth, coupled with a keen awareness of the ecological and social ramifications of their work. One of the most vocal offenders in this regard, despite its avowed goals of objectivity and devotion to truth, is the Committee for the Scientific Investigation of Claims of the Paranormal (CSICOP—SCIence COPs?), founded in 1976 by Paul Kurtz, professor emeritus of philosophy at SUNY-Buffalo. While the attempt to preserve some semblance of rationality in an increasingly irrational world is most praiseworthy, their methods are sometimes questionable (see Appendix I). To give one more example: In 1988 the French immunologist Jacques Benveniste published an article in the journal of the French Academy of Sciences, later reviewed in *Nature*, showing that extreme dilutions of an antibody, prepared by homeopathic means, still had an effect even though there were no traceable molecular amounts of the antibody remaining.[10] Strictly speaking, homeopathy doesn't normally deal with antibodies, but this study seemed to support by inference the methods of homeopathy. CSICOP promptly sent their investigative team (in this case a fraud expert and a stage magician — hardly expert immunologists) in an attempt to discredit Benveniste's findings. As a result, questions arose about the research, which was later corrected and re-verified. The net result was that in the popular press homeopathy took a strong hit while the debunkers emerged as the apparent victors. In the limited circulation homeopathic press, however, it was clearly shown that the research was properly conducted and strongly indicative of its original findings.[11] Did CSICOP publicize Beneviste's newly confirmed results, which lend support to homeopathy, as vigorously as they did their original findings? Not to my knowledge. In another article relevant to this troubling case, Julian Winston cites twenty "scientific attitudes" modified from Bronowski, Diederich, Whaley, and Surrat, which would be well for scientists to keep in mind.[12] Among them are 1) willingness to change an opinion, and 2) loyalty to reality. Scientists, it seems to me, should welcome findings that challenge their assumptions, not attempt to discredit them.

George Bugliarello, then president of Sigma Xi, The Scientific Research Society, leaves us with an open but important question in his editorial lead in *American Scientist* entitled "Five Hundred Years Later:"

> In this century, the full promise of science and technology has still eluded society, in spite of great advances in fighting disease and dramatic improvement in living conditions for many.[13] The carnage of two world wars was made infinitely more terrifying by science and engineering, as are today's many conflicts....The consumer society owes its ultimately unsustainable existence to the techno-scientific ability to mass-produce ad infinitum, way beyond essential human needs. Our hospitals have become impersonal factories, and our cities—the most complex socio-technological systems we have created—an increasing source of frustration and terror.
>
> The spirituality that sustained us in other times or other cultures has been retreating in front of a science and technology unable to fill the vacuum that we have perhaps unwittingly created. As Bertrand Russell pointed out, every time science collided with religion, it emerged victorious. That has been good for science, but a qualified success for civilization.
>
> The time has come to ask ourselves whether we can have a successful future as a species if we cannot reconcile belief with dispassionate search for truth, emotion with artifact, rigor with compassion—if we do not see science in the broadest sense as an instrument capable of transcending its self-imposed boundaries and professed neutrality of belief. As we contemplate the prospect of the next five hundred years, this is the most crucial challenge for science and technology and for society as a whole.

It seems to me that Dr Bugliarello is *pleading* for a science of the spirit.

Science has provided us with a necessary touchstone of rationality in a society which is increasingly flirting with the irrational. The observations of science are becoming more precise and exciting, but that doesn't mean that we should accept the *interpretations* of such data without question. And we should certainly not accept any falsifying of such data (see Appendix I) for the purpose of advancing one's cause. To keep abreast of the wonderful advances of science is highly recommended, provided, of course, we keep the above caveats in mind. And to use our recently acquired reverscope to look at scientific explanations from the opposite perspective can often be equally rewarding.

So, to resolve, or dissolve, this second great cleaver which has been thrust between science and religion, what we have called the "cleaver of incredulity," we have seen that a certain amount of inner work is required. It can never be resolved so long as people sit in one camp or the other taking pot-shots at each other. Nor can it be resolved without transcending the position destiny may have placed us in, and learning to embrace both camps with equal warmth. Both camps are riddled with flaws, to be sure, but at the same time, both camps have much to be commended. And it is on these, the positive aspects, that our attention must be placed as we undergo our personal transformation, our repentance, or metanoien. One camp is calling for repentance, the other for a new paradigm shift, whereas in reality, both are calling for the same thing. They are both calling for a science of the spirit.

John Ruskin, the English author and art critic, wrote in his essay "The Storm Cloud of the Nineteenth Century": "Newton explained to you— or at least was once supposed to explain, why an apple fell; but he never thought of explaining the exact correlative but infinitely more difficult question, how the apple got up there."[14] So, thus inspired, I offer: "The Seed in Newton's Apple" (with thanks to John Ruskin):

> Sir Isaac, sir, please listen to me:
> To eat of your fruit is catastrophe!
> What fell could as well have been a stone,
> a shoe, a jug or some old bone.
> How much more fruitful would your thinking be
> if you had looked up — to the apple tree.

and then you'd have seen, from infinity,
that sap *defies* your gravity!
It's life we're after, not bitter gall,
the only juice from this second Fall.
The apple's alive! alive, indeed,
if we look within, to the living seed.
Joy will return to our cold, stark schools,
when science starts teaching us living rules,
for then we'll learn, contemplatively,
how your apple got up there, in that blessed tree!

Chapter Six

Restitution and Redemption

Once to every man and nation comes the moment to decide,
In the strife of Truth with Falsehood, for the good or evil side;
Some great cause, God's new Messiah, offering each the bloom
    or blight,
Parts the goats upon the left hand and the sheep upon the right,
And the choice goes by forever 'twixt that darkness and that
    light.
Hast thou chosen, o my people, on whose party thou shalt
    stand,
Ere the Doom from its worn sandals shakes the dust against
    our land?
Though the cause of Evil prosper, yet 'tis Truth alone is strong,
And, albeit she wander outcast now, I see around her throng
Troops of beautiful, tall angels, to enshield her from all
    wrong....
We see dimly in the Present what is small and what is great,
Slow of faith how weak an arm may turn the iron helm of fate,
But the soul is still oracular; amid the market's din,
List the ominous stern whisper from the Delphic cave within,—
"They enslave their children's children who make compromise
    with sin."...
New occasions teach new duties; Time makes ancient good
    uncouth;

> They must upward still, and onward, who would keep abreast of Truth;
> Lo, before us gleam her camp-fires! we ourselves must Pilgrims be.
> Launch our Mayflower, and steer boldly through the desperate winter sea,
> Nor attempt the Future's portal with the Past's blood-rusted key.
>
> —JAMES RUSSELL LOWELL (1819–1891), *The Present Crisis*

LET'S ASSUME THAT we have a job to do every day, that we dutifully report to work and do the various tasks assigned to us, and that somehow we muddle our way through the day without the slightest idea of what we're doing or even knowing the end product of our labors or how or why we came to be engaged in such drudgery. Can you imagine how dull each day would be? Most of us probably wouldn't care much about whether the job is done right; we'd just report for work because that's what we have to do.

Fortunately, most of us have a good idea of what our daily jobs entail. But how many of us go through the bigger job of life itself without a clue as to why we're here, what we're doing, where we're going, or what the product of our work should be? Is it any surprise, then, that such a purposeless, nihilistic worldview would lead vast numbers of people to indulge in drugs, verbal and physical abuse, racial prejudices, and all manner of dangerous means to escape? Yet we continue trying to fight wars on crime, drugs, and violence, against evil itself, using largely materialistic means addressing symptoms rather than causes.

Lowell's stirring *Present Crisis* was aimed at abolishing slavery, yet the excerpted lines above pertain to our time as much as his. Slavery has been abolished, at least outwardly, yet its ills persist. Is it not time we recognized the present crisis as a further stage in humanity's ongoing battle against evil, and for our destined place as a community of spirit-beings in a much greater spirit-cosmos?

As children growing up during the terrible days of World War II, we were taught that the enemy were the Germans, the Italians, the Austrians, the Vichy French, and especially the Japanese for their surprise attack on our fleet at Pearl Harbor. It was a prevailing mood of the time to hate the people of those countries. It was only after the war, when I served for three years with the occupation forces in Germany, that I realized it was not the people who were our enemies (the people were wonderful, kind, and cultured), but the pervasive and persuasive swarm of hatred and racial bigotry which had caught both them and us unawares and taken hold of our consciousness for a period of time. Nazism and Fascism were the real enemies, not the people themselves. The real battle was—and still is—being waged on the battlefield of the soul, in the realm of human consciousness.

I felt proud to be an American when I learned of the Marshall Plan. Here we were, spending billions of dollars to help Europe get back on its feet. We were even helping our former enemies. That, to me, was the true "American Dream." The American dream has nothing to do with amassing huge fortunes and living in luxury at the expense of others, as is so commonly touted. That's no dream, it's a nightmare. No. The real American dream is a dream of selflessness, of helping others instead of exploiting them. It's a dream of living in harmony with others of every possible racial extraction, and celebrating our cultural differences rather than exploiting them. It's the dream of the Pilgrims who faced tremendous hardships in their search for freedom from oppression—in short, it's the dream of "do unto others as you would that they do unto you," an admonition that leaves us in total freedom to be ourselves as we pursue our life interests. It is the only dream worth pursuing. And the dream will awaken and pervade reality when we begin to understand the deeper meaning of expressions such as "do unto others as you would that they do unto you," as well as the closely related "as ye sow so also shall ye reap" and similar Biblical injunctions.

These expressions exemplify the *Law of Karma* of Eastern tradition. The understanding and practice of this ancient law of cause and effect, however, degenerated somewhat over the years and is now frequently used as an excuse for laziness: "I can't jump into the lake to save that man. I'd interfere with his karma if I save his life now"—or as a tool for malicious control: "You must do as I say; it's your karma." Accordingly, the teaching of karma was forbidden for almost two thousand years in the esoteric Christian schools so that it could be reintroduced in our time in a more meaningful and accurate form. According to the spiritual scientific investigations of Rudolf Steiner, this censure against teaching the great law of cause and effect came from the very highest source, Christ himself. Christ therefore referred to karma in this form: "As you sow, so also shall you reap," but he did not explicate it. That task had to await our time.

To understand the modern, spiritual scientific concept of karma, we must look at the third great cleaver that separates science from religion; clear, or rational thinking from devout, pious worship. This cleaver is closely related to the first, the so-called problem of evil, which we spent some time discussing earlier. We'll call this new cleaver "the cleaver of perceived injustices." If God exists and is so filled with love as we're told, why are some people born with severe physical or mental limitations? Why are some born into such abject poverty and disease that they have practically no chance of rising above their situation and becoming productive members of society? Why, on the other hand, do some enter this world with immense gifts of genius and robust good health? Isn't it obvious, given such injustices, that there cannot possibly be a God of love?

Some try to answer these questions with platitudes like "God moves in mysterious ways." Others, starting in about the 1960s in some theological seminaries, put forward their version of Nietzsche's "God is dead" theory, which some naturally hesitated to share publicly. Still others simply side-stepped the issue out of weakness and cowardice and became strident fundamentalists: "Have you no faith? You can't question the wisdom of God!"

If the law of karma didn't already exist, then someone would have had to invent it, because it provides the only rational, acceptable answer that remains consistent with all the facts and satisfies the many questions raised by the cleaver of perceived injustices and, indeed, by the Bible itself. But the modern, spiritual scientific concept of karma goes far beyond just answering questions of perceived injustices arising from past behavior. It is a mighty force for the future. Knowledge of karma, as understood and taught in spiritual scientific circles, gives us a whole new meaning to life and lays a foundation of knowledge upon which a sturdy moral and ethical construct can be built. Knowledge of karma, together with its application to our daily lives, is a requirement if we are to have any hope of addressing the question of evil in a meaningful way.

Some Islamic fundamentalist sects have grossly distorted teachings about the "afterlife," the experiences we all go through after death, for the purpose of inciting their youth to unspeakable acts of suicidal and homicidal violence. There simply are not seventy-two virgins waiting in paradise for those committing hate-filled acts like those of September 11, 2001. Rather, the after-death experiences of one who commits suicide are extremely painful and awful to contemplate. As we shall see, this pain is magnified immensely if the suicide also took other lives.

For members of mainstream Islam, it is important that this truth be communicated to the extremists who have distorted the teachings of the archangel Gabriel and twisted them for political gain. It is high time that the vast majority of Muslims who find such terrorist acts abhorrent speak up and continue to do so until "Islam's bloody borders" become peaceful once again. Isn't it time for radical changes to be introduced into a religion suffering such friction with virtually all of its neighbors—Christians, Jews, Hindus, even the peace-loving Buddhists? Isn't it time for everyone, including Western leaders, to realize that every bomb creates more enemies?

In addition to the unspeakable pain suffered after death, those who commit suicide usually find themselves in a much worse condition in the life that follows. We must pay heed to the teachings of spiritual science in these matters. Which seems like the only way this present conflict, promising to be a long and very bloody one, can be brought to a peaceful resolution. The true nature of life after death, reincarnation and karma, must be seriously studied, pondered, and applied to daily life.

But I've been told several times, "Karma, reincarnation—these are anti-Christian ideas." On one occasion, I was forbidden from teaching any more karma courses at a local community college, because the dean had received a letter from a Christian fundamentalist woman I had never met, and who had no idea of what I was teaching. She had accused me and my teachings of being satanic. Letters of support from all my students did nothing to rectify the situation, so I chose not to make an issue of it. Such issues are sometimes better left to a higher court. That higher court is karma.

After passing through the portal of death, we experience a period of "reversed life," during which we relive our earthly lives not only in a reversed time order, but also in a reversed order of sensation. During that time, we experience everything we caused others to experience because of our actions, feelings, and thoughts. This period of cleansing is called Kama Loka, or "place of desire" in Sanskrit ("purgatory" carries too much emotional baggage in the West to be an acceptable scientific term). It lasts about as long as the time we spent asleep while on Earth, about one third as long as our earthly life. While in Kama Loka, all the pain that I inflict on other sentient beings here on Earth will become an equally intense experience for me. Steiner tells us that vivisectionists, too—those who use animals for laboratory experimentation, however noble their aims may be—will experience the same degree of pain they have inflicted on their research animals. Of course it goes without saying that any comfort we give others we also experience with equal intensity. "Love your neighbor as your self."

Now if this were a course in chemistry or physics or some other field of natural science, we would be asked to simply accept what has just been stated in such a matter-of-fact way: If you do this, then that will happen. Okay, that makes sense. Write it down in the notebook, try to learn it, and see if we pass the test. But we're studying holoscopy here, an introduction to spiritual science, and the demands on us, as pupils, are far greater. If we wish to become holoscopists ("holoscopers" might be a better, more active term), we are asked to internalize the teaching and bring it to life in our souls by reviewing it, contemplating it from all angles, comparing it with what we already know, and meditating on it. By no means, however, can we simply dismiss it as being ridiculous or absurd without first subjecting it to such tools, or instruments, of holoscopic investigation. We might ask ourselves, for instance: What is the purpose of Kama Loka? Why would the wise Gods subject us to such punishment in Kama Loka as we may have inflicted on others during our previous earthly life?

At this stage, of course, it would be pointless to ask whether Kama Loka actually exists; we would merely fall back on our prejudices in attempting to answer that question at such an early stage. Answers gradually emerge in the course of performing such exercises. We start seeing, for example, that, as we experience the pain inflicted on others—experienced in all its intensity from our newly acquired higher consciousness in Kama Loka—we naturally want to make amends for that pain. We want to set the record straight and make good whatever evil we may have caused. But we are in a very different condition in Kama Loka than we were on Earth, with no means of rectifying those errors. Consequently, we imbue our souls with a fervent desire to return to "the scene of the crime" to undo all the pain we caused. There is a desire to balance the debits with credits.

But there's more, much more, behind the scenes of karmic law. Further reflection reveals that, despite having made good our evil deed individually, the fact remains that, on a much larger scale, an *evil act* was committed in the universe, or cosmos, even though there may have been restitution on an individual basis. A black mark has been added to the universe because of our evil. As human beings, we have no power to erase that cosmic black splotch, or universal karma. When we think of all the cosmic black marks that have been inflicted on the universe through countless eons and lifetimes of human failings, moments of passion, weakness, and rage, we come to see the hopelessness of our situation. There appears to be no way to climb out from under such a mountain of sin, such a terrible blotch of evil in an otherwise perfect universe. Alone, we are hopeless. We, the children of God, have become sons and daughters of Ahriman, the prince of darkness, doomed to a life of darkness and sin. But we are not alone.

All of this is being observed from the very highest levels of the divine spiritual hierarchies and beyond, from the Godhead, "the Ground of Existence of the Heavens and of the Earth," as it is called in the Creed of the Church of the Christian Community.[1] Human words fail to describe such things, but the divine Word, the Logos, the Son of God, was sent to redeem humanity. Through this mighty cosmic act, this ultimate sacrifice, the universal karma of humanity was erased. Human beings gained the power through this act to ascend in freedom to their divinely ordained position as the tenth hierarchy, the hierarchy of love. The Son of God became the Son of Man so that this majestic cosmic Deed, an affair of the gods, could be accomplished. Freedom means that we choose whether to accept this great gift. Freedom means that we determine whether, as individuals, we will choose to become "the goats upon the left hand" or "the sheep upon the right," as James Russell Lowell reminds us.

For one to say that the teachings of karma are anti-Christian because they contradict the act of redemption merely indicates that such an individual has no idea of the real meaning of redemption in its true, esoteric Christian sense. This specialized area of theological dispute, technically called "soteriology" (the doctrine of salvation through Christ) was an article of faith until Steiner's time, which is why it has been so hotly disputed. Now it can be transferred to the field of knowledge for those who choose to examine biblical teachings in a spiritual scientific manner. Consider the parable of the talents, for example. What could this popular parable possibly mean—that talents are mere currency (1 talent = 60 minas = 3,600 shekels) or that they are one's capacity to perform certain acts with ease and skill, increasing or decreasing according to their use? When we dwell on this mysterious parable in the light of what we have learned about karma, the answer becomes transparent and obvious and verifiable through spiritual scientific research. Suddenly, we see why some individuals are born with prodigious talents in various areas of life, while others must struggle just to feed themselves. The "fortunate" probably (this is no place to judge such people) stretched their soul muscles in a previous life, whereas the "unfortunate" (again, we can only say probably) "hid their talents under a bushel," unused and latent, in an earlier incarnation. Once this great parable is seen in its true light, the cleaver of perceived injustices melts away as the mirage it is.

The only remaining stumbling block for orthodox Christians to an acceptance of karma as a universal world law, affecting all people, is that implicit in this law is the concept of reincarnation. What hints does the Bible give us about this ancient teaching?

As mentioned earlier, the Bible can only hint at reincarnation because it is so closely tied in with the concept of karma, and Christ Himself forbade the public teaching of karma until the beginning of the twentieth century, so it could be reintroduced in a purer form. But the hints are there, and they become obvious once they are understood.

The last chapter of the Old Testament states explicitly: "Behold, I will send you Elijah the prophet before the coming of the great and dreadful day of the Lord" (Malachi 4:5). Then, in the first book of the New Testament: "And as they came down from the mountain, Jesus charged them, saying, Tell the vision to no man, until the Son of man be risen again from the dead. And his disciples asked him, saying, Why then say the scribes that Elias [the Greek form of Elijah] must first come? And Jesus answered and said unto them, Elias truly shall first come, and restore all things. But I say unto you, That Elias is come already, and they knew him not, but have done unto him whatsoever they listed. Likewise shall also the Son of man suffer of them. Then the disciples understood that he spake unto them of John the Baptist" (Matthew 17:9–13, KJV).

Such passages make it difficult for scholars to ignore the question of reincarnation, although the reference is veiled enough so that they could say, "Thus, John is cast into a role like Elijah's...." (*Harper's Bible Dictionary*).[2] And *Smith's Bible Dictionary* makes no mention of the relevant passages.[3] To its credit, however, the *Oxford Study Edition: The New English Bible with the Apocrypha* explicitly states that "verse 13 [of Matthew 17] identifies Elijah as John the Baptist."[4] *The Dartmouth Bible*, goes even further: "This identification of John as the reincarnated Elijah, used by Christians as a proof of the Messiahship of Jesus, is based upon the prophecy of Malachi (3:1 and 4:5) that Elijah would reappear before the 'day of the lord.'"[5] I might add here that Rudolf Steiner's spiritual scientific investigations independently confirm the identity of John the Baptist as Elijah, indicating once again that the Bible is more accurate than the millennia-long accretions of theological dogma and orthodoxy that have been attached to it.

The terms *Purgatory*, from the Latin *purgare*, to cleanse, and *Kama Loca*, Sanskrit for "place of desire," seem to indicate that something more takes place here in this astral realm where we find ourselves after death. It does. This is the soul world, or astral world. In this realm, or level of consciousness after death, we face our habits and addictions and are cleansed of them before entering the true spiritual world, or the Heaven of Christianity. In this realm, an alcoholic, for example, must endure the addictions that were developed on Earth, but now one has no means of fulfilling those desires—gone are the physical organs needed to quench that burning thirst for alcohol. Gourmands, too, find themselves without a palate, and can no longer satisfy their still-powerful, lingering desire for food. In Kama Loca, as mentioned earlier, one goes backward in time until the innocence of childhood is experienced. Only then are we prepared, fully cleansed, and able to enter the realm of the higher spiritual beings. "Unless you become as little children [innocent of all carnal desires] you cannot enter the Kingdom of Heaven."

Three deaths must take place before this can happen: The first is the so-called physical death, where the "I," together with the astral and etheric bodies, lays aside the physical corpse. Immediately after death, the etheric body blazes forth, unfettered by physical integuments, with a panoramic vision of everything that happened during the previous life on Earth. This body bears the memories of every event of that life. This is why it is able to bring all these memories to consciousness. This process, however, usually lasts about two or three days, then the etheric body, too, undergoes a kind of death. It expands to infinity, returning to the etheric or elemental world. This is the second death.

The third death occurs much later, when the astral body, purged of all earthly desires after its sojourn in Kama Loka, is cast aside so that the "I," the eternal human individuality, is able to enter its true home, the land of spirit called "Devachan" in Sanskrit (loosely translated as the Place of the Shining Ones); Christians call this "Heaven." But the word *heaven* carries too much emotional baggage to serve as a useful, technical term, and it is commonly used in a purely physical sense, as in "the stars in the heavens." Hence we use the term *spirit land*, or *Devachan*, in this work. The degree of consciousness with which one enters this effulgent realm depends on the degree of involvement one had with spiritual matters during the previous earthly life. Those who had been occupied with religious matters, for example, will be much more aware than those who spent their life pursuing purely materialistic goals.

In spirit land there are no natural laws. The natural laws of Earth become *moral* laws there. Here we are imbued with what becomes our conscience during subsequent earth lives. It is interesting to note that certain professions have as a sort of rite of passage what could be called anti-initiation. I have heard of anatomy classes in first year med schools, for example, in which students stand around a circle and toss the various organs and members of human cadavers to one another in an effective means of teaching them to treat the human body as mere dead meat rather than as a temple of the spirit. In law school a similar rite takes place when students learn that the practice of law has less to do with truth and justice than with winning. In large corporations, aspiring executives must learn to dance to the tune of the personnel department, pack up everything and, together with their families, move to a different part of the world every few years if they wish to "succeed." This is done with no regard to the soul-destroying effects of such moves on the family and its members. Only by passing such "initiations" are aspirants deemed worthy of "promotion." In the conventional "scientific" practice of farming, successful farmers must learn to ignore a cow whose calf has just been taken from her for the short life of unspeakable tortures necessary to produce tender veal. Ignoring the cries of the tormented mother and the calf, as well as the cries of one's conscience to release the calf back to its rightful place with its mother—these are just a few indications of the hold Ahriman has on modern life.

Speaking of cows, those long-suffering friends of humanity, we can learn an interesting lesson here with regard to the reverscope. Earlier, we learned that animals have their group soul (or their "I," to be precise) in the astral realms. What if the abused and unhappy cow, or the entire bovine group, was to decide that it's had enough of this senseless torture? Many people don't even think in terms of gratitude when biting into a roast beef sandwich—let alone expressing any gratitude verbally. A glass of milk, a bit of cheese, and yoghurt are just commodities to them. What if the abused and unhappy bovine group decided to leave the Earth, that it had paid whatever debts it owed to Earth or to humanity, and then withdrew from further participation in earthly life? It's not too difficult to imagine that veterinarians and scientists would see such a decision as some kind of disease. They would use their wonderful scientific instruments in an attempt to diagnose and cure this "disease." But unless humans learned to love these animals and treat them with the care and respect they deserve, scientists would fail and the bovine group would no longer grace the Earth. Here is another application of the reverscope: to see a phenomenon from two different perspectives, those of the physical and the spiritual worlds. Both observations are correct; it would look like disease from the physical viewpoint, while only the spiritual perspective yields a meaningful interpretation of the departure of the animals. If the present inhumane conditions of animal treatment persist, this example may become more than just hypothetical.

E. F. Schumacher was no stranger to the paradoxical nature of the reverscope, though he didn't use that term. In his popular *Small is Beautiful: Economics as if People Mattered* he says, "When I first began to travel the world, visiting rich and poor countries alike, I was tempted to formulate the first law of economics as follows: 'The amount of real leisure a society enjoys tends to be in inverse proportion to the amount of labor-saving machinery it employs.'" A point well worth pondering.

It may be helpful to look briefly at how the reverscope was discovered. I first conceived it several decades ago as I was contemplating a graphic representation of human progress that was popular then. Time was plotted along the horizontal x axis, and the vertical y axis represented the maximum speeds at which human beings were capable of traveling. It was a logarithmic curve that looked something like this:

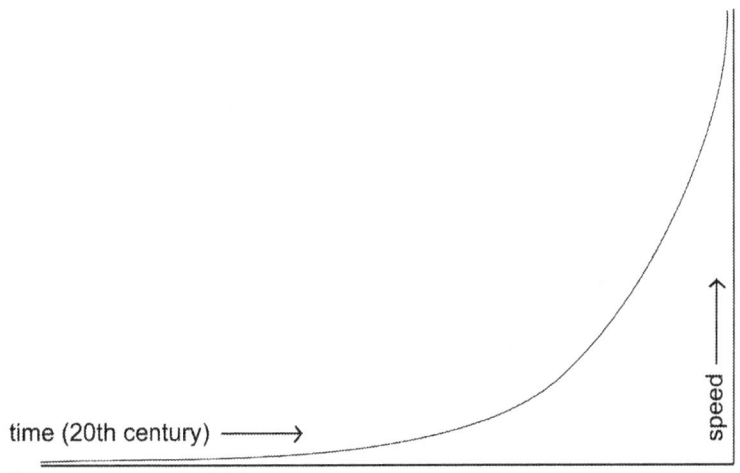

In those days, I was immensely impressed with the seemingly endless prospects of science and technology to carry us into a bold new future. The top of the curve along the y axis ended with the speed of the latest rockets, along with the prospect of much greater speeds to come. How could one not be impressed, even dazzled, with such a breathtaking representation of the accomplishments of the human spirit? I remember showing this curve to many of my friends as we sat, sometimes for hours, contemplating the exciting prospects for a limitless scientific and technological future. Then, one day, something prompted me to contemplate a little further. After all, I said to myself, it's only a convention that speed should be represented in an *upward* direction along the y axis. The graph would be just as accurate, although a bit unconventional, if increasing speed was represented along a *downward* slope:

I immediately noticed how this curve resembled the profile of water going over Niagara Falls, or perhaps better, being drawn into a whirlpool

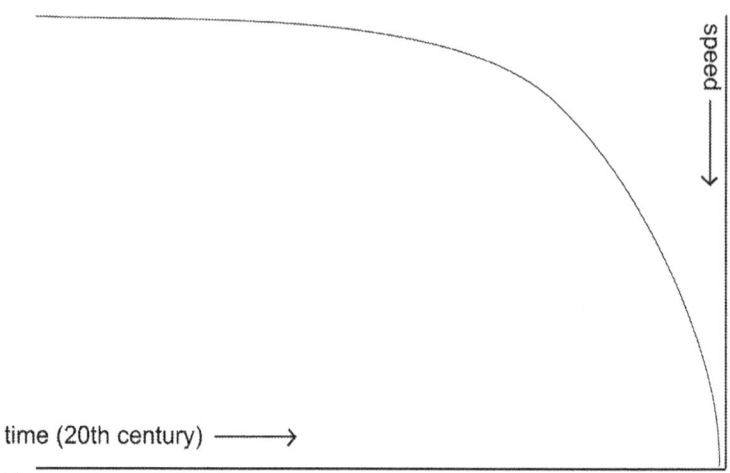

or abyss similar to Devils Hole, a huge, permanent maelstrom about three miles downstream of the Falls. I began to speculate about the possibility of applying the reverscope to other phenomena. After all, it soon seemed obvious that it was more than just a harmless convention to represent increased speed in an upward direction; it is a bias, hidden and deeply-rooted. Both representations are equally valid, though one implies advancement and progress, while the other, because it descends, suggests failure and decline. It became obvious, too, that increased speed could just as well have been represented from right to left, rather than left to right, but I'm sure you get the point.

I looked at organization charts. There, at the very top, free as the air, was the chairman, the board of directors, and the CEO. By mentally inverting such charts, I noticed that it was equally valid to see such people as having burrowed downward, more deeply into the corporate morass, and hence they were really not free at all. As people burrowed down more deeply along the corporate ladder, I saw them not becoming freer but increasingly enmeshed and entangled in the sinister webs of corporate politics as well as the snares of increased ethical and moral temptations. Of course, many corporate leaders are well equipped to withstand such temptations.

Thus was born a powerful perceptual tool, the reverscope. Years later I discovered that Steiner already knew of it, though he didn't use that term. He used a more rigorous and far-ranging approach: projective geometry. He encouraged his students to apply themselves, as an exercise, to this exciting area of mental and artistic endeavor.

So what does all this have to do with the question of evil? By exercising and stretching our capacities to see things from many different equally valid perspectives we gain the capacity to transcend the subtle but powerful biases hidden in conventional views of the world. Until we have overcome such biases, we cannot become truly free. And evil can be vanquished only in freedom. "And the choice goes on forever 'twixt that darkness and that light," to harken back to Lowell's stirring words.

With a sincere application to the study of the laws of karma and reincarnation—by really bringing them alive in our souls—we can then reach such a state of transcendent perception that the third great cleaver separating science and religion, the cleaver of perceived injustices, can be seen for what it really is: a mirage. From this perspective we see that they are not injustices at all. There is, in fact, immense wisdom and great cosmic laws operating behind the scenes with the birth of every child. It is no accident or injustice but, in many cases, the result of past deeds that some are born with great capacity for success, while others are born hobbled and crippled and severely limited.

But woe betides if we should attempt to judge such souls from our purely human level of perception, for there are many other laws, too, that operate behind the scenes in such matters. We have no way of judging what a particular individual may or may not have done in a previous life to bring about, say, a severely debilitating mental or perceptual problem. Within the anthroposophical community, there are many individuals and groups who have made it their sacred duty to work with such "souls in need of special care," treating them with the utmost care, dignity and love. After all, what appears as an incurable case of mental retardation in one life may in fact be simply a stepping-stone to immense genius in the next. Such great souls may have chosen to suffer in this life so that they can develop the soul forces needed for far greater tasks in the future. The lofty words of the Beatitudes take on an ever richer meaning in this regard: "Be ye therefore merciful, as your Father also is merciful. Judge not, and ye shall not be judged: condemn not, and ye shall not be condemned: forgive, and ye shall be forgiven: Give, and it shall be given unto you" (Luke 6:36, 37 KJV). Another perfect rendering of the law of karma.

Steiner tells us that during our epoch there will be many false messiahs. We have already seen gurus who have proclaimed themselves lords of the universe and such. A few years ago, a small group of people took out full-page advertisements in large metropolitan newspapers around the world, proclaiming the return of Christ in a physical body. Fortunately, we were suitably warned (see appendix 2), and no damage was done. But when will the real Christ reappear?[6]

In his remarkable 1995 book called *I Am with You Always: True Stories of Encounters with Jesus*, G. Scott Sparrow gives numerous depictions of encounters with a being of immense love and wisdom who brought comfort and solace and sometimes a whole new direction to people in all walks of life. What surprises me about this book is that it was written by someone who apparently had little or no knowledge of what Steiner had to say about this subject; yet it verifies Steiner's predictions exactly—that Christ would appear to increasing numbers of people beginning in the early 1930s. It must be emphasized that this reappearance is not physical but an etheric phenomenon. The Mystery of Golgotha, as the pivot point on the huge fulcrum of earthly evolution, can occur only once on the physical plane, but, as mentioned earlier, that divine intervention changed for all time the course of Earth evolution. Now, during our time and with increasing frequency for thousands of years to come, an intimate, personal encounter with the Savior, with no less than Christ himself, will be possible for people all over the world. I can bear witness to this; my own encounter occurred at the darkest, most desperate time of my life.

It was in the morning of Good Friday, 1969, although Good Friday and Easter meant nothing to me then. I had just left my wife and children less than a year earlier and was leading a life of wanton abandon as a bachelor. I was alone that morning, lying in bed and reading, when I became aware of a presence in the room. I experienced an immediate clairvoyant contact with this great luminous presence. He could see right through me. He knew me so intimately that he knew what my thoughts were before I could think them. He saw all my flaws and excesses, my arrogance and lack of belief, and yet he loved me in a way that is impossible to describe. For a few precious moments I could do nothing but lie there, basking in that divine infinite love. But then, all too soon, I too became aware of all my faults and shortcomings; a cesspool of seething demons—of selfishness, lust, arrogance, and addiction to pleasure. I was ashamed. I wanted to hide from his gaze and from that deep, pure, penetrating, and illuminating love. Lying there in my bed, I was in agony, utterly permeated with shame. I felt unworthy to be in his presence. So I did the only thing I could do; I begged him to leave me alone, and he disappeared just as quietly and mysteriously as he had come.

Until now, I was able to tell this story to only a few people. But, in addressing this important question of evil, it has become necessary to stand and be counted as one of his witnesses. I am still a sinner, although I would like to think that my transgressions of coffee and cigars are far less frequent and less damaging than those of that earlier time. I certainly don't wish to imply that I am now "saved" because of this experience. I can only say that he left me in complete freedom. I was free to continue my life as I had been doing, in which case I probably would have self-destructed long ago. I was free to simply ignore the experience, to push it out of my consciousness and pretend that it had never happened. But I was also free to start searching for a path that would lead me out of my condition of sin. I needed a path of *knowledge*, one that would answer the many lingering questions that somehow the church seemed unable to answer. Later on that year, I was introduced to anthroposophy.

If I were to be examined by ten or a hundred conventional psychiatrists, they might tell me that I was suffering from delusions when I had this vision. Nevertheless, I would be able to quietly and confidently assure them that it was no delusion. The experience I had on that lonely and desolate Good Friday was far more real than any experience on the physical plane of consciousness. A deep, penetrating *knowing* existed and was being offered to me if I chose to accept it.

So now I can say with complete confidence: Christ lives! And we are now living in the time of his long-awaited reappearance.

Chapter Seven

The Afterimage

Here we need to be wise.
If you can understand, figure out the animal's number,
because it is a number for humans (to reckon).
His number is 666.
—The Revelation of John, 13:18

After almost two hundred years, people are only now beginning to appreciate that Goethe was a great, insightful *scientist* as well as one of the world's greatest poets.[1] The credit for much of this appreciation goes to a young man who, toward the end of the nineteenth century, was asked to edit Goethe's scientific writings for the definitive Weimar edition of the collected works of Goethe. The young man had just been awarded a Ph.D. in epistemology (the theory of knowledge, or the philosophy of science), and he eagerly took on this daunting task. In the process, he wrote voluminously of his findings. That young man was Rudolf Steiner.

Goethe's greatness—as well as his relative obscurity as a scientist—stems in part from his unorthodox methods of observation. Rather than speculating a hypothesis and then setting out to prove it, Goethe let the phenomena themselves speak. This requires immense discipline and the holding back of even the slightest preconceptions or prejudicial impulses. Formulating a hypothesis, after all, is not the first step in scientific investigation. One must, in utter honesty, ask: Where does the hypothesis come from? A brief look at Goethe's inspiration for his study of light is helpful here.

In his book *Catching the Light,* Arthur Zajonc writes, "One evening while at an inn, Goethe noted the entry of an especially beautiful young woman. Her white face was radiant, contrasting strongly with her jet-black hair. A scarlet bodice shaped her ample figure to advantage." (p. 194). I'll leave the rest for you to enjoy in the original. The point is that, when the lady stepped out of the bright light, an afterimage of her complete figure against the white wall behind was seen where she first stood. The afterimage was complete in every detail, except that it was a reversed image of the original. What had been black became white and vice versa; the scarlet bodice became a beautiful sea green. Rather than dismissing this as an optical illusion or as "mischievous phantoms of the mind," Goethe chose to use it as the starting point and basis for his study of light, which he eventually called *Farbenlehre,* or theory of color. Anyone can easily repeat this experiment by staring at the same spot of a color picture in bright light for about thirty seconds, followed by either closing one's eyes or looking at a white sheet of paper. We will return to this phenomenon of the reversed afterimage later, though in a somewhat different context.

As discussed earlier, one of Steiner's subjects for contemplation is "Wisdom lives in the light." This rather enigmatic expression tells us nothing until we draw out what is hidden behind the words. We must penetrate this saying; we must surround ourselves with it until we are elucidated by its wisdom. To do this we could sit quietly each day for a certain period and repeat it as a mantra until it yields its hidden meaning. We could also do the same thing, but with the aid of what we have gained through spiritual scientific study. This second course is far more productive, but to follow it we must touch briefly on additional areas of spiritual scientific research in an attempt to illuminate the meaning, or some of the meanings, of the pregnant expression "wisdom lives in the light."

Spiritual science teaches that, like human beings, the Earth experiences a series of reincarnations. During Earth's three earlier embodiments, conditions were very different from those in the present, the fifth, embodiment. Perceived physically, the first was a body of warmth that also became luminescent. The second was a kind of air form, and the third added the watery element. It was not until the fourth stage, the Earth proper, that hard, dense, solid matter congealed onto the physical plane. Looking to the future, there are three more incarnations, each ascending gradually back to a more spiritual effulgent, or luminescent, state. Hindu traditions speak of a long period of human evolution referred to as Kali Yuga, or dark ages. One of the functions of this eons-long descent into darkness, the so-called Greater Kali Yuga, is that human beings are placed in a condition in which they must assume—in total freedom and of their own volition—responsibility for their own evolution. Some will find the necessary spiritual resources within themselves to make the ascent with ease. Most, however, will find it to be a great struggle, and in that struggle we will gain new capacities and talents and greater insight to understand what it means to live in, and to outgrow, darkness, nihilism, and sin. A tableau presented itself to me after working a while with the meditation "wisdom lives in the light"; it was an ages-long descent from light into darkness and a subsequent ascent back to the light. During the fourth incarnation, that of the Earth itself, our evolving planetary organism first recapitulates the three previous incarnations and then enters the fourth, the Atlantean Epoch. We are now living in the fifth great epoch, the "Post-Atlantean," which is in turn divided into seven smaller "cultural" epochs, each lasting about 2160 years, of which this again is the fifth.

Here I am running counter to Steiner's injunction that spiritual scientific truths should not be presented in an over-simplified manner. The danger, of course, is that people may think they understand them, whereas they may have grasped only the briefest sketch. The foregoing description is definitely an over-simplification.[2] Nevertheless, I take responsibility for these sketchy words, because they are needed to set the stage for what follows.

Returning to earthly evolution proper, it is not difficult to see a gradually gathering dark age in the Earth's recapitulation of the larger cycles of its previous incarnations, culminating in its densest phase, that of the Atlantean period. Now, during the fifth great epoch, the post-Atlantean, we encounter yet another dark age that began about five thousand years ago and ended about a hundred years ago. This is called the Lesser Kali Yuga and is especially significant for earthly evolution. During this "dark night," a mighty event occurred that changed the destiny of human and earthly evolution; the Earth took on the capacity and potential to become a star. Spiritual scientific investigation tells us that, at that precise moment, the earth's etheric and astral bodies were instantly transformed and purified. A pivotal point occurred the moment Christ's blood touched the Earth; the Mystery of Golgotha had begun. A bright, cosmic light entered the darkness of Earth and instantly transformed its entire nature. That deed, however, had to be accomplished in such a way that it would not interfere with human freedom. It had to be enacted in a remote place, far from any big city where historic records or "proof" would be kept; otherwise, it would have interfered with that freedom. This was the second revelation that came to me as a result of living with the beautiful mantra "wisdom lives in the light." It revealed the wisdom of Christ, who appeared in the midst of that great darkness, the Lesser Kali Yuga.

Turning to an even smaller scale, we see the cycle of the year, the annual emergence of the light of full summer from the cold darkness of winter, only to return to that darkness. In the midst of this darkness, we celebrate a festival of light, an inner light, symbolized by the lights on the tree and the flaming Yule log. Such a festival would have a different meaning if it were celebrated at any other time of the year. Another insight into "wisdom lives in the light" is found in the text of the South American oratorio *Navidad Nuestra* (our Christmas), with words by Felix Luna:

> The Three Wise Men
> The Kings are arrived,

> And they are three—
> Malchor, Gaspar, and black Baltazar.
> They bring Him
> Honey, boiled wine,
> And a white poncho of llama wool.
> Good little boys and girls,
> Sleep,
> Malchor, Gaspar and Baltazar are here.
> They will leave you gifts
> To play with
> Upon waking in the morning.
> The child God thanked them,
> Ate the honey,
> And wrapped Himself up in the poncho.
> And, Afterwards,
> He looked at them,
> And the sun lit the midnight skies.
> (translator unknown)

To speak of a midnight sun is quite absurd from an outer, materialistic standpoint, but students of initiation science are quite aware of its important inner significance.[3]

There are yet more insights to be gained from contemplating "wisdom lives in the light." There are probably many more, but this one pertains to the subject of evil. It, too, is profoundly inward and mystical if we can only picture ourselves as seeds lying dormant in the cold dark earth. Seeds do not have to see the sun when they respond to its springtime dawning, nevertheless they are quickened by its hidden forces. We, too, as living seeds, can sense the dawning light outside, beyond the dark, as we respond to this light from within our hearts. This Christ within, as Paul put it, can have a powerful resonance with the macrocosmic Christ. This exercise, practiced daily, can help offset the devastating effects of the violence and carnal impulses of our modern, materialistic society and help us start the germinating process needed to come to terms consciously with evil.

The autobiography of Jacques Lusseyran tells the heart-warming story of a young man who, though blinded at the age of eight, was nevertheless able to lead a group of resistance fighters ten years later against the horrors of Nazi occupation in France.[4] His positive attitude and child-like purity of soul allowed him to "see," to develop an inner light that served him flawlessly as he went about his many daily tasks. The life story of Jacques Lusseyran gives a completely new meaning to "wisdom lives in the light."

Attempts to decipher that great occult work, *The Revelation of John*, from the perspective of conventional scholarship have proven largely futile. Indeed, they have bordered on the dangerous. Witness the recent episode of some irresponsible and probably paranoid group of people who convinced many others that a soap company was hiding the number 666, the number of the Beast, in one of its labels. This caused a great furor in certain circles, while the soap company had to defend itself, at great expense, against irrational charges and redesign its labels. Such irresponsible behavior does nothing to mend the rift between science and religion. And unfortunately there are zealots in both camps who take great pleasure in using explosive remarks to deepen and widen that schism. One task of spiritual science is to provide a perspective that sees no such chasm, but only an illusion brought on by a materialistic infestation of all three of those equally necessary fields of human endeavor: science, art, and religion. For society as a whole, a balanced development of these three fields is just as important as is the harmonious, balanced development of thinking, feeling, and willing in individuals. President Kennedy knew that the feeling nature of society—the sphere of art and culture—had been neglected; in 1962 he declared, "I see nothing more important for this country than full recognition of the arts."

In chapter 4, we looked at one artistic representation of the two poles of evil in our discussion of Steiner's pastel called *Licht und Finsternis* ("Light and Darkness"—see front cover illustration). There is another, even greater representation—a huge wooden sculpture over ten meters

The Group –*This colossal tribute to Christ, taller than the average house, was conceived and executed by Rudolf Steiner with the assistance of English artist Edith Maryon*

high called *The Group*. Between depictions of Lucifer and Ahriman, its striking central figure is the "Representative of Humanity," the Christ. His left hand is raised, and his right is shown in a conscious downward gesture; he stands not in defiance of these two inimical powers, but in a gesture of blessing and benediction. It is a gesture of love. As a result of his Presence, Lucifer withers and falls from his lofty heights while Ahriman, a bony, leathery figure, becomes tethered and powerless in his grotto below, enchained by the gold he so greedily amassed. Fortunately, when the first Goetheanum was destroyed by fire on New Year's Eve 1922, this masterpiece of mystery knowledge was unfinished in another building and had not yet taken its intended place at the rear of the stage, where it surely would have been incinerated. It was thus saved and now occupies a special place in the second Goetheanum, for all to appreciate and study.

Lucifer and Ahriman are not our only adversaries; we have yet to look at the Beast. But before we could investigate what spiritual science has to say about the mystery of the Beast, the mystery of 666, it was necessary to introduce a simplified version of the prehistoric cycles of time as seen by the seer, or initiate. Now we must look more closely at our own great epoch, the post-Atlantean. As mentioned, it is divided into seven smaller periods of a little more than two thousand years each, called "cultural epochs." The first three cultural epochs were those of the ancient Indian, the ancient Persian, and the Egypto-Chaldean-Babylonian-Assyrian. They were characterized by an increasing objectification of human consciousness, culminating in the fourth, the Greco-Roman, in which human consciousness had become so attuned to the physical plane that the Greeks could produce their wonderful statues and architectural masterpieces so admired even today. The present fifth post-Atlantean cultural epoch is, in a spiritual sense, a recapitulation of the third, Egyptian cultural epoch, but with a higher potential. The sixth in turn will echo the second, while the seventh will mirror certain aspects of the first, while carrying forward the fruits of previous incarnations.

The Greco-Roman epoch began in 747 BC and ended in AD 1413; like the others, it lasted for 2160 years, or the time it takes the Sun to precess from one sign of the zodiac to the previous one. We are said to be living in the Piscean age, while the previous epoch was the age of the Ram, or the Lamb in esoteric Christian terms. The "Lamb of God" (Christ) was to have taken on physical form at the midpoint of the Greco-Roman period, but just as humans have their demons, a demon also represents the exact opposite of the Lamb. Inner facts of evolution dictated that this demon, the beast with two horns, would appear in AD 666. This event would have had catastrophic consequences for humanity.[5] To counter this fateful intervention, the Mystery of Golgotha had to occur 333 years before the mid-point of the fourth cultural epoch.

What would have been the effect of the Beast's appearance in 666 had the Christ event not occurred 333 years earlier than the mid-point? We would have become geniuses; we would have been *given* the wisdom that the creator Gods intended human beings to *earn* through life experiences. We are not scheduled to earn that level of perspicacity until the fourth millennium, more than a thousand years from now. The real danger of receiving this premature wisdom would have been that future human progress would have been truncated, and we would have been unable to further develop our higher spiritual nature. The effects would have been devastating for proper human evolution. Just as the true Sun God, Christ, has the power to give to humankind the forces for redemption if those forces are accepted, so too does the Beast with two horns, the false ram, have the power to give human beings all that cancels out Christ's influence in us. Now, thanks to Christ's great offsetting power, we are free to choose the path we will follow. Humanity is separating itself into two: a good and an evil race, just as the Bible predicted [Matt 25]. The task of the Beast with two horns, called Sorat, is to pull down the portion of humanity that rejects Christ and to expedite the separation. Sorat is the mightiest demon in our solar system. People under his influence will utter terrible blasphemies and we "will not be able to believe that they are really human beings. They will develop in a very strange way—even outwardly. They will be intensive, strong natures outwardly with fierce features and a destructive rage in their emotions; they will have a face in which one will see a kind of a beast's face outwardly. Sorat men and women will also be recognizable (inwardly); they will be those who not only ridicule spirituality—they will also fight it in the most terrible way, and they will want to thrust it down into a cesspool."[6]

Every 666 years since his original attempt, Sorat tries again. Around the thirteenth and fourteenth centuries, it was notably the Knights Templar who suffered at his hand because they wanted to reestablish Christ in human thinking as the true Sun God, the Sun Genius. Now, 666 years later, in the twentieth and the twenty-first centuries, we are experiencing another onslaught of the Sun Demon Sorat.

Theologians have written so much about the Antichrist that, even in a rather large tome, it would be difficult to summarize their writings fairly. The number of conflicting views nevertheless makes it clear that they are merely "shooting in the dark" at whatever goes against their particular religious views. For them any opposing view represents the Antichrist. For example, one traditional, and very conservative, theologian treats the subject from a Catholic perspective and sees the Antichrist as anybody who does not blindly accept the strict teachings of "the Magisterium," the Holy See, the Church, the Pope. The author condemns Protestants and Jews alike as being the Antichrist, even though this major work of almost 300 pages bears both the *Imprimatur* and the *Nihil Obstat* of official sanction. He is particularly severe in his branding of the Catholic universities as being inspired by the Antichrist, inasmuch as they are too liberal and have diverged from the strict teachings of the Papacy.[7] After reading this priest's work—a painful task!—it becomes obvious that only spiritual scientific insight into the true nature of the Antichrist offers meaningful insight about this great threat to humanity.

Are we ready, are we strong enough in our spiritual knowledge, to withstand the onslaughts of this terrible blaspheming Sun Demon—the Anti-Christ, the evil, opposite afterimage of the true Sun God, the Christ? Are we mature and knowledgeable enough to tread a path of moderation between all the strident, cacophonous fundamentalist ideologues of every stripe, which have become so vocal and numerous in today's confusing times?

Chapter Eight

Mysterium Magnum

> There is one thing [which we should inscribe anew into our souls every day]...that in this Fifth Post-Atlantean period the human being must be a warrior for the spirit.
>
> —Rudolf Steiner
> *Secret Brotherhoods:*
> *And the Mystery of the Human Double*

> This above all: to thine own self be true,
> And it must follow, as the night the day,
> Thou canst not then be false to any man.
>
> —Shakespeare, *Hamlet*

To be true to one's self implies first knowing one's self. While this may seem a simple task, self-knowledge takes a lifetime—or, rather, many lifetimes. Who am I? Where did I come from? What am I doing here? Where am I going? Such questions have been the bane of philosophy since its inception. Yet they must be answered if we are to have any hope of applying meaning, purpose, and direction to our lives. Only then can we experience the real and lasting buoyant enthusiasm needed in our struggle out of life's morass. And what a morass we're in. What a lovely mess we've made of things. Greed and self-interest have been the primary human motivators. As a result, we blindly pour toxic chemicals on our land in an effort to promote life. We minutely examine genes, chromosomes, and DNA in a quest for another Shakespeare or Einstein.

We pour billions of dollars into the "war against crime," with virtually no effective thought about what causes crime—or war or disease or the seemingly endless array of other ills that beset humanity. The answers are always "just around the corner." We live in a time of pandemic delusional insanity, and one of our most dangerous delusions is that we believe we are sane and healthy.

In an insane world, the voice of sanity is considered insane, which seems to be the case today. It's "delusional insanity" because we've been deluded into thinking that we are perfectly sane and that civilization is pretty much the way it should be. Yet isn't it essential that we make a serious attempt to hear the healing messages of truth, beauty, and goodness? The first small step in this direction is to garner the strength and courage to improve our thinking. In this regard, I draw your attention to several books.

Felipe Fernández-Armesto, a professor of modern history at Oxford, calls for a completely new university department devoted to examining the concept of truth. In his *Truth: A History and a Guide for the Perplexed*, he draws on his vast knowledge of anthropology and history to illustrate how different cultures treat this important goal.

Two decades earlier, John Wilson, from Oxford's Farmington Trust Research Unit, sounded a similar note. His book *Language and the Pursuit of Truth*, however, approaches the question more from the perspective of linguistics. He cautions us that, before we can correctly assert a truth, we must first understand it and then understand how to verify it properly and, finally, have good evidence that it has been verified. Back in my advertising and PR days, I was guilty of several misdemeanors in this regard. I was just too lazy to get the facts straight before writing about a client's product or, while ad manager of a manufacturing company, our own product. I simply accepted what I was told to say without questioning deeply enough.

Psychiatrist M. Scott Peck's *People of the Lie: the Hope for Healing Human Evil* is a wide-ranging, very popular work that ascribes lying to psychological causes, which he calls "malignant narcissism." Dr. Peck's courage and selflessness in attempting to get at the root of the problem of evil are quite praiseworthy.

In *Seven Experiments That Could Change the World: a Do-It-Yourself Guide to Revolutionary Science,* Rupert Sheldrake urges modern scientific thinkers to closely examine and, indeed, perform experiments in seven areas that could bring the prevailing materialistic worldview into serious question. The first has to do with stay-at-home pets getting excited the moment their master or mistress *decides* to come home, long before they actually do arrive. The second studies homing and migration patterns in wild animals. The remaining five involve insect colonies as superorganisms; people becoming aware of being observed from behind and even turning around in response; the phantom-limb phenomenon of amputees; the accuracy of so-called mathematical constants; and whether competent scientists allow their beliefs to influence their data. Readers of *Trust Us, We're Experts,* cited earlier, will already realize the seriousness of this problem.

In addition to these books, we could recommend a study of the "sleeping prophet," Edgar Cayce, and his remote healings. How did he do it? There are dozens of books on the subject, such as *Divine Interventions: True Stories of Mystery and Miracles That Change Lives* by Dan Millman and Doug Childers. Also interesting in this regard are attempts to prove that thinking is not restricted to the brain, as some materialists think—for example, Courtney Brown's *Cosmic Explorers,* a fascinating look at what he calls scientific remote viewing. Closely related to this would be the study of those who have had spontaneous out-of-body and near-death experiences. Many works attest to such phenomena, but few reductionist scientists bother to look at them at all because they don't fit their own comfortable, materialistic worldviews.

These works, and of course many more, are aimed at healing the evils in today's society. Some writers, on the other hand, contribute to societal ills by means of their purely reductionist thinking. We are now prepared to do battle, not with the authors themselves but with the nihilistic, reductionist thinking they promulgate. We could call these people *catechists,* people who, using their books of irreligious instruction, prepare the unwary for worship in the 'Temple of Ahriman,' the Temple of Deception. What surprises—and pleases—me is that this battle, this exposé of materialism, is such a joyous one. See if you don't agree.

Before we enter the temple though, a few words are in order: Ahriman's rightful domain is that in which things can be weighed, counted, and measured. We are therefore *always* in his realm so long as we are conscious on the physical level of experience. Christ calls him *the Prince of this world.* And indeed he is that, and more. But now, as we enter his subterranean grotto, his sanctuary, we shall arm ourselves with the light of Christ consciousness, somewhat akin to the lamp miners or spelunkers wear on their helmets. Everywhere we look we will cast light on the wrought work of Ahriman. We will not encounter him directly, though, because he cannot tolerate the light we bear; the light of *Gnosis,* or spiritual knowledge. Be assured, he will scurry off into the shadows, finding refuge behind his many icons and statues. Nor can he approach us from behind, because our footprints themselves consist of light; the light of *enthusiasm* we have for this adventure.

The following works were chosen not only because their authors are well known in their fields, but also because the books are brilliantly written and worthy of serious study, though they stem from a materialistic and reductionist worldview. One is the work of a philosopher of religion; the second was written by a well-known biologist; the third by a zoologist; and the fourth by a physicist. This latter work we will examine in some detail. But first, on to a professor of religion and philosophy at Luther College in Iowa. We encounter his work in the narthex of the temple of Ahriman.

His name is Loyal Rue and he presumably teaches religion, yet he is an uncompromising atheist and nihilist. He feels that nihilism—the theory that the universe is blind and aimless—is indisputable. From this premise, he constructs his book *By the Grace of Guile: The Role of Deception in Natural History and Human Affairs,* a marvelous testimonial to the intellectual achievements of our time. I am not being sarcastic when I praise these works. I recommend them most heartily to anyone who really wants to come to terms with their compelling arguments and the relentless, scholarly pursuit of their goals. If you accept their premises, you are almost compelled to accept their conclusions, because their arguments are so finely honed. And they are fascinating and exciting to read in their own right.

Rue leads us through a comprehensive history of deception in human affairs, as well as in nature. From optical illusions to the use of camouflage in biology to a history of deception in religion, psychology, and philosophy, we can easily be persuaded that deception, guile, and lying are natural, even desirable, subterfuges for us to employ as healthy, productive human beings. Because Rue's personal cosmology includes no God, he proposes placing what he calls a "noble lie" [*Sic!*] before the people—a lie that is wholly consistent with the latest findings of modern science. In other words, since God doesn't exist according to modern establishment thinking, we'll create one. We'll create a God that science cannot quibble with, and thereby we will reunite science and religion. How will this lie be introduced? How does Rue suggest that the lie proposed in Germany, let's say, would not be significantly different from that promulgated in the U.S.? He proposes a world federalist government, a *New World Order* [check the Internet for many references to this] of scientists, academicians, and other elitists who would create and oversee the acceptance of the "noble lie." I swear, I'm not making this stuff up. And we're paying good money in tuition expenses to send our kids to high priests like Loyal Rue? (You can see why I'm tempted to Spoonerize his name.) So there, in the narthex, before even entering the inner sanctum of Ahriman's temple, we see the warning plaque: "Noble Lie." We have been suitably warned. At least he has the honesty to tell us he's lying; a fascinating seeming-paradox which would require a book-length treatise to explore fully. But that is not our task today. Let's just accept the warning at face value as we begin our exploration of this intriguing Temple of Deceit!

In a way, it's too bad for Rue that Lyall Watson, our second author, didn't come out with this next book a little sooner; he could have saved Rue a great amount of research. Watson's *Dark Nature: A Natural History of Evil* would have contributed immensely to Rue's data, although Rue certainly didn't need Watson's 1995 findings to bolster his already strong arguments. Unlike the previous author, Watson doesn't seem to feel any need to construct a great *deus ex machina* [*diabolis ex machina?*], or a "noble lie," to save humanity when his discoveries lead him into a dead end. As a biologist and ethologist who studies animal behavior in an attempt to understand that of human beings, he simply writes what he has studied and observed personally on his ocean-going trawler, *The Amazon*, while traveling around the world.

From this enviable perspective, Lyall Watson has been able to make some very significant contributions to the study of evil—at least from a reductionist perspective. For years, he has carefully observed how various species habitually manifest particular behavior patterns toward their close relatives, behaviors that differ significantly from the way they act toward strangers (or toward those from a different genetic pool) of the same species. These observations led him to develop what he calls his "principles of pathics," which operate on the genetic level in a ruthless, calculating way. Just as ethics is the study of "good" behavior, pathics is the study of evil but, according to Watson, this evil is encoded genetically. Simply put, it consists of three premises he has observed and confirmed in nature: 1) Be good to "insiders" (those of the same genetic pool); 2) be nasty to "outsiders" (same species, but not related); and 3) cheat on your mate. By following these three simple pathic rules (I will refrain from calling them pathetically simple rules), Watson shows how the entire course of evolutionary history has progressed up to humankind. Strongly implicit in this concept is the notion that there is little or nothing we can do about it. Evil just is; we have to live with it. Yet, he says, "We are the world's first ethical animals, at the mercy still of our biology, but capable also of rising above it." There's the hope. Watson often calls for the "Goldilocks effect," the path of moderation, or Aristotelian Golden Mean, in our dealings with evil. But, alas, all he seems to leave us with is what we could call the "Pandora effect." The box has been opened, the meanies have escaped, and all we're left with is hope. Watson's work can be greatly admired; particularly his valiant efforts to come to terms with what makes humans tick and what makes evil click. But to make the Goldilocks effect work, we must first know *where* to establish that Golden

Mean. It is not somewhere between humans and evil as Watson suggests, but between the two extremes of evil itself; that is where we are. Only spiritual science can show us where we must stand on that continuum. As Sun-tzu put it in his classic, *The Art of War*, "Know your enemy and yourself and your chances of winning are a hundred percent. Know only yourself and not the enemy, and your chances are even." Nevertheless, it is fair to ask whether we really know our selves. Therefore, I would add to Sun-tzu: "If we don't know ourselves (what it means to be human in the deepest, most spiritual sense), we have no chance at all."

Lyall Watson's work is built on that of such people as Richard Dawkins (*The God Delusion; The Selfish Gene; River Out of Eden;* and *Climbing Mount Improbable*) and Desmond Morris (who views human beings as "naked apes," human animals living in "human zoos").[1] These people meticulously gather and assess their data, getting high marks for scholarship to be sure, but their reductionist perspective always leaves us hungry for something more. It's as if our bellies are full but somehow we don't feel nourished—beautifully contrived and packaged junk food for the mind. While I am reporting here only on English-speaking authors, similar work is being carried out in other countries, in other languages. These people may be correct in their arguments, but—and here's the spiritual scientific bombshell—they are correct only from a materialistic perspective. Human beings did not descend ("ascend" might be more apt) from the apes; rather, from a spiritual perspective, apes and other animals descended from the human being.

Rudolf Steiner, after carefully studying the works of Darwin and Haeckel, foresaw the dangers of blindly pursuing this one-sided perspective on human evolution, with its focus on our animal rather than our spiritual nature. He foresaw, perhaps, the eventual formation of a world federalist government, whose task it would be to promulgate the big lie, the "noble lie," just to keep human beings content and happy on the sleepwalker's treadmill to a materialistic oblivion. In his spiritual investigations, therefore, he asked to see the spiritual realities of this evolutionary process. He asked this of the good gods—mighty, beneficent beings whose task is to nurture human development along a course that is proper and productive. He presented the results of his observations in important works such as *An Outline of Esoteric Science* and *Cosmic Memory*. Careful study of these and subsequent works will show his spiritual findings to be wholly consistent with Darwin's material discoveries, with the exception that Steiner's interpretation of these discoveries from the spiritual perspective is infinitely more productive and meaningful than materialistic interpretations or theorizing could ever be.

Our third author, Matt Ridley, also examines genes, but he comes to startlingly different conclusions than those of Watson. This is typical whenever reductionism is the sole approach. You're able to prove pretty much whatever it is you set out to prove, even with the same evidence. His *Origins of Virtue: Human Instincts and the Evolution of Cooperation* is far more optimistic than Watson's but only slightly less reductionistic. Ridley traces the billion-year "coagulation" of our genes into cooperative teams (i.e., organisms) and the million-year coagulation of our ancestors into cooperative societies. In his view, cooperation and ideas about it lead to virtue; the alternative would lead to extinction. Ridley arrives at his conclusions through game theory, the prisoner's dilemma, and other reductionist techniques (which we needn't review here). These are fascinating intellectual games, but nonetheless reductionist.

So, what about Loyal Rue's "noble lie" (what an oxymoron!)? It will probably look something like this: In his *The Physics of Immortality: Modern Cosmology, God and the Resurrection of the Dead*, Frank J. Tipler gives us two books for the price of one. The first, almost 400 pages long, is for the non-specialist, while his appendix for scientists consists of more than 100 pages. According to the author, "To comprehend it all [the appendix for scientists] without reference to a research library would require Ph.D.s in at least three disparate fields: 1) global general relativity, 2) theoretical particle physics, and 3) computer complexity theory." Well, never mind—the first part alone of this carefully constructed work is well worth the price, and is quite understandable to most people.

Tipler begins with the premise that, in order to do the physics of the far future (the book's focus), we must regard "all forms of life—including human beings—as subject to the same laws of physics as electrons and atoms. I therefore regard a human being as nothing but a particular type of machine, a human brain as nothing but an information processing device, the human soul as nothing but a program being run on a computer called the brain. Further, all possible types of living beings, intelligent or not, are of the same nature, and subject to the same laws of physics as constrain all information processing devices" (from the preface). Maybe I'm missing something here, because I don't have three Ph.D.s in those fields of knowledge and wisdom, but when Professor Tipler describes a human being in that way, this particular "machine" feels impelled to quietly point out that he is not describing a human being at all, but rather precisely what human beings are *not:* he is describing a corpse.

Tipler goes on to tell us how arrogant physicists are because their predictions are generally true. "In my previous publications on religion and physics, I have attempted to conceal this arrogance [not very successfully] {His self-assessment, not mine.}. In this book, however, I have not bothered, mainly because such concealment in the past has prevented me from presenting the strongest case for reductionism. And reductionism is true. Furthermore, accepting reductionism allows one to integrate fully religion and science." He concludes his preface with this: "It is time scientists reconsider the God hypothesis. I hope in this book to persuade them to do so. The time has come to absorb theology into physics, to make Heaven as real as an electron."

It would be difficult for me to do justice to the amazing construct that Tipler builds upon such premises without rebuilding the entire book with him. Let's just say that he postulates a perfect condition, the omega point, reminiscent of Pierre Teilhard de Chardin's, which transcends time and space and from which our phenomenal universe is guided. Tipler's omega point, however, exists only in a super computer of the far future. He even discusses the problem of evil and resolves it with his omega point theory, as well as a computer-generated "savior" intended to satisfy some of the concepts of Christianity. He has clearly spent a great deal of time and scholarly effort in his attempt to subsume the whole of theology into a branch of physics and thus "reunite" science and religion. If Rue's "Noble Lie" plaque is displayed at the entrance of the temple dedicated to lies, then Tipler is the high-priest at the altar. Once again, high marks for scholarship and forceful reasoning, despite his absurd premise. But there are more absurdities to come.

The "immortality" aspect of Tipler's scheme stems from his belief that once you're dead, you're dead—finished. But, in his view, some super computer in the far future will replicate all the genes that ever were and, Presto! you will be miraculously brought back to life because a replicated you is *you*; there will be no difference. You may be living inside a computer, but you won't know the difference. You'll think you're in paradise, because the computer will create exactly the kind of environment you want. Of course, a moment's reflection shows us that identical twins, exact replicas of each other, are two distinct individuals, thereby putting the lie to Tipler's dreams of immortality in a machine. He apparently has no conception of the true human condition—that we are all unique spiritual beings.

To avoid the ultimate death of the Earth millions of years in the future, Professor Tipler envisions sending tiny von Neumann (self-replicating) probes out into space to propagate the entire universe with our genetic pool. The propulsion system for these probes calls for a huge 250-gigawatt (250 million kilowatts) laser, in orbit around the sun, to accelerate the probes, each of which would require a "sail" eight kilometers across to capture the light beam. The laser itself would require a solar collection area "of about 40 kilometers square." But wait, there's more. To focus the laser beam on the rapidly departing probe (traveling at about nine tenths the speed of light) would require a "huge Fresnel lens, one billion kilometers in diameter." That's larger than the diameter of the sun. Now I have a small plastic Fresnel lens, about ten *inches* across, which refuses to stay flat. Professor Tipler may be a great physicist, but he sure ain't no engineer! The scary part of this is that he's deadly serious. He totally ignores such problems as deceleration from such relativistic speeds, as well as reentry (entry, in this case) and a host of other sticky little details, leaving them, I suppose, to the *deus ex machina* of his almighty supercomputer of the far future.

Rudolf Steiner admonished us to become warriors for truth, for the spirit, but he never told us that this royal battle with Ahriman would be such great sport.

There you have it; one of contemporary science's latest academically acceptable "noble lies." Our choice is easy; we can continue to pursue a materialistic science based on false premises, or we can pursue a spiritual science based on reality. We are very much at the crossroads with this one. Powerful spiritual beings have been unleashed to tempt and goad us into continuing our materialistic path toward a sleepwalker's paradise, which in reality would mean complete devastation for humanity. We cannot ignore these potent entities. Courageously facing these beings reveals the awful consequences of such a choice. What, one may ask, can spiritual science promise us? Hard work! After all, it stands to reason and experience that the highest goals are achieved only through the hardest work. But, I must add, there is no drudgery in this work; it is the most joyous work imaginable. It is a joy to gradually discover who we are, where we come from, why we are here, and where we are going. This is the great mystery, the *Mysterium Magnum*. It is the joy of knowing that we are working not out of selfish hope for personal salvation, but to lift all of humanity. It is the joy of working with other, similarly inspired human beings to present not a noble lie based on deceit and treachery, but rather the noble truth, which is based on a humble, honest search, filled with awe and wonder at the marvels of the universe and its wisdom-filled schoolhouse, our Earth.

God is not dead; he has merely retired behind the door so that we as his prodigal children might rediscover him in joyous reunion, a joy beyond all earthly description. The tools for this quest are at hand: the implements of holoscopy, crude and imperfect as they are at this early stage, and the refined instruments of an initiation science, a science of the spirit, which are offered to us in all their perfection by a true master craftsman who devoted his entire life in patience and self-sacrifice to make them available. Only through initiation, Christian Initiation, and through quiet, inner work can the door be approached properly and safely. Then we can knock and wait in humble expectation to be deemed worthy of having the door opened to us.

Chapter Nine

Thoughtworthy Themes

A Player, Not a Pawn
Blame no one but yourself
when your day goes all a-wrong.
In this turbid game of life, then, you'll
become a player, not a pawn.

For if you rail against your fate,
thrusting blame in fortune's face,
then you might as well give up.
You've already lost that race.

Or, should fortune smile upon you
like a skittish brown-eyed fawn:
Seize it! Then thank your angel;
as a player, not a pawn.

For we are *co*-creators
in this blessed game of life.
We who call down blessings.
We who drum up strife.

When you can see, and thank, the Wisdom
in *all* that comes along,
then you'll know the joy of being
a player, not a pawn.

It would be wrong for me to leave you with the impression that all modern scholarship is based on false premises. Many who feel they are being pushed increasingly to the periphery of the mainstream nevertheless work diligently to bridge the abyss and honestly reconcile the latest scientific findings with a spiritual worldview that is sane and reasonable. One such, from the religious perspective, is Joseph Fletcher, whose *Situation Ethics* (though easily misunderstood as being a poor excuse for slovenly behavior if not read carefully) reveals itself to be a thoroughly uplifting system of ethics that leaves us free.[1] Further, the theodicy he advocates, his attempt to resolve the problem of evil, accords fully with the findings of spiritual science. It is based on the "tutelage theory" of William Temple and Josiah Royce, the theory that God provides evil, which drives people toward moral levels they would never reach without struggle, sacrifice, and wrestling with evil.[2] Steiner states it thus: "We could even say that the wise guidance of the world allowed humans to become evil and gave them the possibility of doing harm, so that in repairing the harm and overcoming the evil they can become stronger in the course of karmic development than they would have become had they reached their goal without effort. This is how we should understand the significance and justification of obstacles and hindrances."[3]

Such words bring to mind the parable of the Prodigal Son, alluded to in the previous chapter. They help us understand why the father in the parable was so much more pleased with his returning sinful, prodigal son, after a life of wild abandon, than he was with the dutiful son who hadn't been strengthened through overcoming great obstacles and temptations. Christ is not advocating evil in this parable, he is evoking the wisdom-filled process that gives evil purpose and meaning.

In ancient times, the holy wisdom that guided human development from within the mysteries was protected by stringent rules and regulations. Candidates for initiation had to experience and pass rigorous trials and temptations before they were allowed access to the inner sanctum, the Holy of Holies of the mysteries themselves. Those who didn't honor the code of secrecy were punished with death. It was said of Aeschylus that he was put on trial for illicitly divulging mystery wisdom in his plays. His only defense, which saved his life, was to prove to the temple priests that he had never been initiated and thus could not have violated an oath he never took.

In many ways the modern mysteries are just the opposite of those of pre-Christian times. They are no longer hidden away in a temple and accessible to only those few who had been invited to undergo their perilous ascent. The word *reverscope* stems, not only from the word *reverse*, but also from *revere*; for without reverence everything most valuable escapes our notice. And the great, quintessential reverscope, Christ himself, blew the walls away from those ancient holy mysteries that had served humanity well for eons; he instituted a whole new dictum: Love one another as I have loved you. Gone were the ancient "thou shalt not" commandments, replaced by the law of love, the single new commandment. What is good and proper in one epoch becomes evil in the next. If we continued to follow the dictum "an eye for an eye, a tooth for a tooth," a law that is now dispensed from higher realms as the law of karma, our world would soon be populated by blind, toothless ideologues. Gone is the insistence on personal salvation; in its place is the great leaven for all humanity—to love one's neighbor as one's self. Today's holy mystery is found, not sequestered away in a hidden temple high on a mountain, but in the deepest recesses of the mystery of the first person singular, present tense, indicative mode of the verb "to be." It is the Mystery of the Word, or Logos, of the Christ himself—the mystery of the I AM. In today's mysteries, guru is now spelled "Gee, you are you!"

The "I" is the eternal spirit within each of us that differentiates the human kingdom from the animal, as discussed earlier. It gives human beings an upright posture and vaulted brow. It is not to be confused with the "I" in "I sat down." Indeed, our language would be better served spiritually if we had some kind of a construction like "My sat down" (meaning the body) or, perhaps better, "I sat myself down," making it reflexive. Perhaps the most accurate way, considering the constraints of the language (designed as it is for physical phenomena) would be something like the awkward "I sat my body down."

I raise this problem to show the difficulty that spiritual investigators have in translating their observations into everyday language. A completely new mood of soul is needed to study spiritual science, and serious students must learn to go beyond the limitations of the language to the spirit behind the words. Comparatively few seem ready and willing to do this. While this is sad, it also protects modern initiation wisdom from the profane. Those who divulge today's secrets are no longer put to death as was the case with the Ancient Mysteries. That's because the new Mystery Wisdom consists of 'open secrets,' simply scoffed at or, more likely, just ignored by those not prepared at this time to enter into them. Unfortunately, to keep heart and mind divinely open tends to be particularly difficult for highly trained professionals, regarded as experts in their respective fields. They too must "become as little children" and instill in their souls a sense of awe and reverence for the divine manifestations around them.

For *all of us* this process is difficult, because it requires a complete re-examination of all we have accepted as true. It means *testing* our old, familiar ideas, and throwing out the worthless and harmful ones. And it means undergoing inner upheavals and re-organizations that ultimately transform, not only our customary soul mood, but the very constitution of the soul itself.

Of course, people don't have to change professions to undergo this change. Oprah Winfrey, for example, must have awakened one morning and realized that she was part of the problem, not the solution. She had been promoting the sleazier aspect of human nature on her popular TV show before suddenly realizing that she was in a position to be a powerful force for the good, precisely because of her show's popularity. Since then she has focused on the positive and the good, to great effect. Apparently she saw through the rather spurious argument used so often by the media: "We're not promoting violence [or whatever vice *du jour*]; we just show what's already out there." Curious, isn't it, how television touts its awesome powers of influence when pitching to perspective advertisers, yet it claims to have absolutely no influence when accused of wreaking havoc on society with its endless parade of violence, sleaze, and sexual perversion. It's time to recognize ethics and morality as more than the purview of preachers. Preaching about morality is, for most, a real turn-off. We don't want to be told what to do, based on a set of precepts that date back to a pre-historic past. That's one reason why today's modern consciousness requires a scientific basis for matters that were previously restricted to the world of religion.

Many well-meaning and responsible scientists are attempting to bridge the gap between science and religion. One of the most notable efforts is by Henry Margenau and Roy Abraham Varghese, as related in *Cosmos, Bios, Theos*.[4] In this book, sixty leading scientists, including twenty-four Nobel Prizewinners, answer six basic questions about the origin of the universe, Earth, and humankind. As well, they offer their views on the existence of God. I mention the twenty-four Nobel laureates only to show that these are serious, firmly established scientists in their fields, and not to out-do Professor Kurtz (see appendix I). After all, truth is not democratic, and belief in something by millions of people doesn't necessarily make it true. This work is well worth the effort for anyone who may still feel that science today has totally expunged God from its intellectual worldview; it powerfully demonstrates that this is not the case. Most of the contributors have unique views, so they would be difficult to summarize here. Nevertheless, there are a few observations that stand out. Arthur L. Schawlow of Stanford University strikes a truly holoscopic note when he says, "The context of religion is a great background for doing science. In the words of Psalm 19, 'The heavens declare the glory of God and the firmament showeth his handiwork.' Thus scientific research is a worshipful act, in that it reveals more of the wonders of God's creation." What a beautiful picture he gives us! A scientist approaching the laboratory bench with the same reverence as a priest approaching the altar.

Wolfgang Smith of Oregon State University reminds us of a universal truth: "What the scientist [like everyone] needs in the face of the religious phenomenon is a profound humility. To understand what religion is, one must first of all be religious oneself; the essential thing simply cannot be known from the outside."

Margenau, a distinguished physicist in his own right, is certainly to be congratulated for his monumental work in assembling the thoughts of such a large number of prominent scientists. *Cosmos, Bios, Theos* should serve as a strong bulwark against the ungodly forces of a materialistic worldview.

Most religions as they are preached these days do not meet the minimum standards of intellectual integrity demanded by serious thinkers, who, in their honest pursuit of a meaningful worldview, cannot accept the dictums of blind faith. On the other hand, many sciences as they are practiced today do not meet the minimum standards of ethical behavior that require science to step back from its myopic, reductionistic world view and take a serious look at its long-range effects on human beings and the Earth.

Here is an exercise whose value lies in the fact that it sits squarely in the middle ground between both camps. It calls for both intellectual integrity and a strong sense of responsibility to the Earth. I call it the "living seed exercise," and it is based on a similar exercise in Rudolf Steiner's *How to Know Higher Worlds*. Take a seed; any seed will do, but it should be capable of germination in your area. Next, imagine that you have an imaginary artificial duplicate seed made of porcelain, and glazed so skillfully that to physical sight it looks identical to the real seed.

Now place the living seed before you and concentrate on this thought: If I planted this seed in the ground a plant would grow from it. Focus your attention on the imaginary plant. Continue studying the seed; obviously, there is something about this living seed that the ersatz seed lacks, something hidden from my physical sight. Now comes the salute to thinking; through the force of thinking an invisible quality in this seed has made its presence known to me. In other words, your thinking has led you to the inescapable conclusion that there is something as yet hidden in this living seed which the dead, fake seed does not have; a life, or etheric, force. Steiner then carries the exercise further, showing how we can develop the sensible/super-sensible faculty of actually seeing this force, but for our purposes we don't need to go that far. I cite this exercise here simply to demonstrate that intellectual integrity, honest thinking, leads us to the inexorable conclusion that there is an invisible, super-sensible world of etheric or life forces. Can biologists, people who supposedly study life, look at two seeds and tell us which will germinate and which will not? I have yet to meet one. Yet if we work to develop this new capacity to actually "see" the life forces in a seed we will be taking a major step forward in developing a wholesome, new science of life, a new living Biology.

Some people may find that, by quietly gathering evidence against certain practices in their particular place of employment or type of business, they can become a powerful influence for good by being whistle-blowers. This hasn't always been easy, but now, fortunately, there are whistle-blower laws designed to protect such people from incrimination, and even reward them. We have seen the positive results of whistle blowing in the tobacco industry, the Internal Revenue Service, the nuclear energy business, and the FBI with the revelation of all manner of cover-ups and manipulations. FBI agent Coleen Rowley has become a real twenty-first century hero in the eyes of many. Because of her honesty, the FBI has undergone complete reorganization, as has the Homeland Security Department. Perhaps, with time, similar revelations will arise from other areas of human endeavor. If so, it will seem to some that civilization is going through a period of chaos, even catastrophe. The old established institutions will be shaken to their roots, while the new emerging ones based on truth may not yet be readily visible. Consider what the Catholic Church is going through because of the recent attention to stories of sexual abuse by some of its priests. Isn't the Church undergoing profound changes because of these revelations? This should not alarm students of spiritual science; it is the natural emergence of the consciousness soul, the development of which is a primary task of this our fifth post-Atlantean cultural epoch. It involves the sometimes painful task of bringing to consciousness much that has remained hidden for many years. It is a preparation for the sixth cultural epoch, which begins about fifteen hundred years from now, when, according to spiritual investigation, evil will no longer be able to hide.

What does it mean to say that evil will no longer be able to hide? Those today who persist in evil and choose not to make the necessary efforts to transcend lust and greed and other lower, carnal impulses will be unable to disguise their intentions in that not-too-distant future. Their faces, bodies, and gestures will out-picture the ugliness and evil of their untransmuted lower natures. The human kingdom will have continued in a process that is already apparent to those who have eyes to see; there will then be a separation into two races, one good, and the other evil.

To the degree that we dwell only on our own problems and ignore those of others, our problems will begin to loom ever larger and more menacing, demanding more of our time and effort. But, on the other hand, if we devote our lives to helping others and assisting them in time of need, then our own personal problems will seem to diminish by comparison. Look in the typical bookshop today. There are hundreds of "self-help" books, but how many are designed to inspire and show us how to help others? Look around; for every Mother Teresa, there are thousands, perhaps millions, who are concerned only with their own lives and problems. I'm not advocating that we all become like the late Mother Teresa—hers was a unique destiny—but I do advocate spending time thinking about what we see around us. Look at those hard-driven, world-harming individuals who lust after power; at the slothful, pleasure-seeking lovers of ease. Then compare them to those who devote their lives to helping others. You'll see that pleasure-seeking hedonism refutes itself. Those who devote their lives to seeking pleasure are often the least happy and fulfilled, the least wholesome and healthy. By learning to help others we begin to relegate many of our own troubles to the compost heap where they belong. Look at today's popular schools of so-called psychotherapy that encourage us to blame others and pamper ourselves, to dwell *ad nauseam* on catering to the "inner child" in order to improve our self-esteem, while ignoring the real source of self-esteem—to get on with life and accomplish something worthy of esteem. It is not the inner child we should be catering to but the inner sage, the Christ within.

I cannot end this book without stressing that it is merely a handful of seeds, a few of which I hope will be carefully tended. When the concept of karma, for instance, germinates in the soul, it can be seen as a powerful foundation for a system of ethics with which to countervail the evil within and the evil without. I am aware that I may be accused of being as much prescriptive as descriptive, and I make no apologies for that. After all, the purpose of studying a disease is to eradicate it, and certain prescriptions may be indicated. I am also aware that this work is incomplete. We didn't discuss the secret brotherhoods, for instance, a subject on which Steiner had much to say.[5] Those who feel drawn to such impulses should be advised that the use of occult powers to influence other human beings, even with good intentions, belongs to the "left-hand" path of evil; it's a matter of trying to play God. It is a path of manipulation and deceit and is not recommended. We discussed the consequences of manipulation and deceit earlier in this work.

Further, we have not discussed the double, or *Doppelgänger*, a curious alter-ego-like inner influence that functions in some more than in others.[6] An adequate treatment of that subject is beyond my capabilities and expertise. This question perhaps belongs more in the field of psychopathology, and serious inquiries in this matter should be addressed to competent anthroposophically trained physicians.

Just as wolves are necessary to the health of a caribou herd, evil is necessary for healthy human progress and development. It "trims the herd," so to speak, keeping us wary and on our toes. It is dangerous for caribou to ignore a wolf, and similarly we must remain vigilant, as we have attempted to show here, lest we succumb to the many wiles and temptations of our clever adversaries. We *need* the challenges of evil to grow and evolve. Just as important, we may now begin to understand that without evil the marvel of human freedom would not exist.

Humanity has come of age; we have reached a stage of development at which our emerging individualities have ceased to heed ancient exhortations and the stern commands of "thou shalt not." We are apprentice gods and, as such, we must learn to test the spirits ourselves to see whether they are good. This is a healthy mode of consciousness and need not lead to painful prodigality. After all, the wise learn from the mistakes of others; while fools fail to learn even from their own; and the holoscopist aspires to become a wise person. By looking at evil and at life itself as holoscopically as possible, as we have attempted to do in this short dissertation, we begin to see and realize that many of the ancient exhortations are worth heeding. One of our great tasks is to rediscover that wisdom, not as patriarchal commands but as freely held knowledge.

In our pursuit of such wisdom, we have tried to show that, for those whose intellectual quests have led them to a materialistic worldview, the time has come to accept the fact that there is a path to the spirit that is wholly consistent with the highest standards of intellectual integrity. It leads to wholesomeness and soul hygiene, both for the individual and for society. Those who embrace one of the many orthodox bodies of faith must inescapably conclude that the frequently contradictory teachings of all those bodies cannot all be correct. People can no longer be satisfied with embracing a faith simply because they were born into it or because they were converted to it at an earlier age. Every sect has its slavish adherents, yet mathematically the chances that any one belief system embraces all the truth are, at best, only 1 in X, where X is the total number of such systems. Intellectual integrity forces us to accept the probability that other systems may have at least as much truth as our own, and that they are therefore worthy of equal consideration. Dogmatism, in any form, is thus shown to be the result of slovenly thinking. We have seen that there are dogmatic scientists too, equally capable of creating havoc through blind adherence to their 'Gospels.'

The time has come for scientists to practice reverence for the truth. It is time, too, for pious believers to test their faith with the same exactitude, precision, and clarity employed in the highest and best of scientific traditions. In short, the time has come to realize that there is a path to the spirit called spiritual science, and that such a path must now be utilized if we are to survive our unavoidable encounters with the evil that seems more pervasive today than ever. To assist our efforts in this, we have also attempted to show that the three great cleavers, the great wedges, that have separated science and religion for so many years, are no longer valid. The first cleaver, the so-called problem of evil, along with the other two, the cleaver of incredulity and the cleaver of perceived injustices, simply no longer stand up under the light of modern spiritual scientific investigation. Once it is seen that these cleavers have lost the power to separate science and religion, it will no longer be *de rigueur* for scientists to espouse atheism, nor will it be necessary for the so-called creationists to formulate a questionable pseudo-science in a vain attempt to bolster their interpretation of the scriptures.

Thus regenerated and made whole, science and religion can now join hands with their beautiful sister, the arts, whose task is to portray spiritual realities in a sense-perceptible form. Together they begin to weave a tapestry of truth, beauty and goodness, a fabric made of science, art, and religion in equal measure, which not only warms and protects us from Ahriman's frigid enticements, but also enthuses us to work together in harmony and love and freedom. We thus fulfil the mission of evil by understanding it and learning to cope with it in ourselves and in others.

In the final analysis, this book is as much about freedom as it is about evil. Freedom is not an ephemeral phenomenon—a brief moment of bliss based on some response to an external situation—it is a state of mind available to anyone willing to exert the effort. It is the ability to make a conscious decision to do a good thing, knowing that one's decision is not impelled by any unconscious force, external or internal. Then, when our moral and ethical decisions are made in complete freedom and confidence, we will be able to say:

"I used to be afraid of the dark. Now, the dark is afraid of me."

Epilogue

Redeeming the Apple

Is the apple evil? The Romans seemed to think so. So too did the Bible, if you believe the myth that the fruit of the "tree of knowledge of good and evil" was of the genus *malus*. Apple lore is replete with suasive nuances of both evil and good. We "upset the apple cart" when we foul someone's plans. An "apple bed" is short-sheeted as a joke to prevent one's legs from being fully extended, forcing the weary individual to get up and remake the bed before enjoying a good night's rest. On the other hand we have such expressions as "the apple of my eye." In Australia, "She's apples" tells us that everything is hunky-dory. Johnny Appleseed helped pave the way to the West by planting apple trees along the path in that fine old American legend. And what could be more inviting than mom and apple pie?

Let's trace briefly the descent of this ubiquitous fruit through the ages and see if, perchance, it might show us a glimpse of an upward path as well. We've mentioned the apple's purported role in our first "Fall," our descent into matter. But there was a second fall as well involving this tempting treat that is not yet widely recognized: the fall of Isaac Newton's famous Apple. Here we are led below the realms of nature into the cold, calculating realm of nature as machine. Newton didn't "discover" gravity. Gravity was known for eons—ever since the first human beings felt the press of earth on the soles of their feet. What Newton did discover, with the aid and inspiration of his legendary bump on the head, was to show us the way to calculate the effects of gravity on everyday objects. Thanks to Newton, we can now calculate accurately the trajectories of projectiles and the paths of free-falling bombs. But is the apple to be blamed for this? No; this noble fruit played a *passive* role in this descent, as it did in the first. In the first case, the apple magnanimously allowed its name to be yoked in myth with humanity's descent from the etheric cosmos into physicality. In the second case, Newton's apple figures poignantly in our further descent into gravity's universe, and the valley of the shadow of the death of light; the realm of the calculable. Once again, the sweet and long-suffering apple became our 'fall guy.'

As you read, humanity is falling a third time, falling deeper into the crackling kingdom of electromagnetism, into the yawning chasm of the 'lower abyss,' into the realms where our old friend, Mr Ahriman, holds total sway. Yes indeed, we now have a third fall on our hands, in which the name of that old forbidden fruit figures prominently, mysteriously.

For centuries we thought we were building *upwards*, towards a towering civilization dependent on technology and electromagnetism. But our reverscope shows us an altogether new perspective; it reveals us to be tunneling ever *downward* with the help of our increasingly numerous, evolving machines. The twentieth century saw massive scientific and technological breakthroughs into the ahrimanically-pervaded domains underlying the material world. These ahrimanic breakthroughs culminated not long ago in the rise of the personal computer and the creation of the World-Wide Web. What a stroke of bittersweet, cosmic humor it was, to yoke the long-suffering ever-hopeful apple to the first widely used and universally celebrated PC—the Apple Computer!

Thanks to the miniature computer, we now have smart bombs and electronic warfare, cell phones, iPods, and all the other miniature gadgets of twenty-first century life. But wait! As denizens of these new-found territories of the mind, we must realize that we are not mere slaves in Mr. Ahriman's evil land. Vast new powers are available for us here—for good or evil. Consider that open heart surgery has become almost routine, thanks to the many available high-speed electronic life-saving devices. And computer-driven lasers flawlessly burn away excess tissue in ophthalmic procedures barely dreamed of twenty years ago. How many other marvels might we mention! What a wonderful time this is to be alive! Talk about the apple of our eye.

But let's return to our long-suffering scapegoat whose fruitful course through history has provided us, not only a globally recognized symbol for descent, but also a glowing symbol for possible rebirth and re-ascent—for a bright new future—the lowly apple. Cut crosswise, all apples reveal a five-pointed star, the beautiful pentagram, a graphic representation of the number five. Five is truly a mystery number. In *Occult Signs and Symbols*, discussing the pentagram and pentagon, Rudolf Steiner tells us:

> Five is the number of evil. This will become clear to us if we again consider human beings. In their development human beings have become fourfold and thereby beings of the created world. Here on Earth, however, the fifth member of their being, the spirit self, will be added. Were they to remain fourfold beings, they would be constantly directed by the gods—toward the good, of course—but they would never develop their independence. They have become free through the gift of their germinal fifth member, but it is also from this that they have received the ability to do evil. No being can do evil who has not arrived at 'fivefoldness.' Wherever we meet with evil, such that it can actually adversely affect our own being, there a fivefoldness is at play.

Some people consider the Pentagon in Washington, DC a symbol for evil. But if we "stellate" the pentagon—extending each of its lines in both directions, we obtain the five-pointed star or pentagram, a high symbol for earthly and cosmic humanity, which shows up, wondrously depicted, in the famous drawing by da Vinci usually referred to as "Vitruvian Man." Much has been written on this subject, and much more could be said about the occult significance of the pentagram, but none could say it better, or with more authority, than Rudolf Steiner who, in one of his Christmas lectures states,

> Finally, all that permeates the cosmos is present in human beings and is symbolized in the pentagram at the top of the tree. The

deepest meaning of the pentagram may not now be mentioned, but it is the star of humankind ... the star that all the wise follow, as did the priestly sages in ancient ages. It symbolizes the Earth that is born on the Night of Consecration, because the most sublime light radiates from the deepest darkness. Humanity lives on toward a state when the light shall be born within, when one significant saying shall be replaced by another, and when it will no longer be said, "The Darkness does not comprehend the Light," but when the truth will resound into cosmic space with the words, "Darkness gives way to the Light that radiates toward us in the star of humankind, darkness yields and comprehends the light."

So! Here we have hidden within the apple a real mystery. It is a magnificent representation of the quintessence, the fifth element, which represents both humanity at its current stage of development, and the mystery of evil.

To press the metaphor a bit further, what do we do when we have a superabundance of fresh fruit, when the crop is ready for harvest? We make apple juice. And how is this accomplished? The good juice is pressed out of the virtually useless pulp. A primal scission must take place dramatically in order to accomplish this. No! *The* primal scission, the culmination, the decisive final moment for the apple. No longer does the apple as such exist. The Bible calls it the separation of the sheep from the goats, but this analogy is fenced in by limitations of field. After all, goats are useful critters, too. Pulp, on the other hand, can be saved only for a second pressing or as compost. Other than these, it is useless compared to the fragrant, delicious, and nourishing fresh-pressed juice. Which would you choose to be?

The moral? If we love apple juice, must we not also love the pulp from which it was expelled? And let us not forget—there are precious seeds hidden in that "worthless" pulp. Perhaps one day we'll even learn to appreciate the press itself, that primal vice from which all other vices are derived.

Appendix I

Committee for the Scientific Investigation of Claims of the Paranormal (CSICOP)

In 1975, a group of 186 "leading scientists" (that's how they billed themselves), including eighteen Nobel laureates, signed and published a statement in *The Humanist* (Sept/Oct), then edited by Paul Kurtz. Their purpose was to attack astrology. Later that year, it was reprinted as a booklet by CSICOP with the title *Objections to Astrology*. By this time, the list of signatures had grown to "192 leading scientists, including nineteen Nobel Prize winners."

This was quite a noteworthy event. Rarely do we get even ten or twelve scientists willing to sign a statement on a controversial topic. Yet here we have 192 of them! It's probably the nearest thing to a unanimous statement that modern science has yet produced. One would assume that they had all made a thorough scientific study of astrology before committing their names to such a document. Or is that merely a naïve assumption? Their *Objections to Astrology* included such "scientific" observations as, "Now that these distances [from the earth to the planets and stars] can and have been calculated, we can see how infinitesimally small are the gravitational and other effects produced by the distant planets and the far more distant stars." Now, just because gravity obeys the inverse square law, does this mean that all the other effects must obey that law, too? Does it prove that astrology is invalid? These humanists seem to think so.

To continue, astrology "can only contribute to the growth of irrationalism and obscurantism." I suppose that if you make an "ism" out of something, it sounds more menacing. These objections were drafted by Bart J. Bok, the late emeritus professor of astronomy at the University of Arizona and past president of the American Astronomical Society. He goes on to say in an accompanying article: "Before the days of modern astronomy, it made sense to look into possible justifications for astrological beliefs, but it is silly to do so now that we have a fair picture of man's place in the universe." In other words, not only have these "leading scientists" not studied the subject about which they are pontificating, but professors Kurtz and Bok consider it silly to do so. I'll leave you to judge who is contributing to "irrationalism and obscurantism."

My point? If science is the disciplined pursuit of truth it claims to be, then many scientists today are simply not scientific enough. If these humanists could only develop reverence for truth instead of simply mocking others' beliefs, they might be more successful in their efforts at science and more respected by those who, although serious and extremely intelligent, are not necessarily scientists of their ilk. My purpose here is not to defend astrology; I'm simply pointing out some highly questionable areas of thought on the part of the humanists. This is particularly distressing because it is precisely such humanists who so actively tell the rest of us how we should think.

H. J. Eysenck and D. K. Nias, who seem to be real scientists, state the case much better than I could in their *Astrology: Science or Superstition?*[1] They give Paul Kurtz and his Committee for the Scientific Investigation of Claims of the Paranormal a polite slap on the wrist for the way they treated the French statisticians Michel and Francoise Gauquelin. These two researchers published their findings about certain astrological correspondences in the birth charts of more than fifty thousand subjects, which they had carefully studied and analyzed. Eysenck and Nias had to say this about the Kurtz Committee's attack on the Gauquelins' work:

> We have looked carefully at the arguments concerning statistical evaluation and experimental design, and we have inspected with great interest the debates between the Gauquelins and their critics [Kurtz *et al*] on various points. We have come to the definite conclusion that the critics have often behaved in an irrational and scientifically unusual manner, violating principles they themselves have laid down, failing to adhere to their own rules, failing to consult the Gauquelins on details of tests to be carried out, or failing to inform them on vital points of the results. We have not found any similar misdemeanor on the part of the Gauquelins, who seem to have behaved throughout in a calm, rational, and scientifically acceptable manner, meeting criticism by appropriate reanalysis of the data, by the collection of new data, however laborious the process might have been, and by rational argument. We do not feel that the "scientific" community emerges with any great credit from these encounters.

Note how Eysenck and Nias formulate their thoughts in a balanced and objective fashion and how their carefully worded indictment of Kurtz's committee is all the more effective and believable because Eysenck had thoroughly studied his subject before writing about it—a practice Kurtz and his friends would be well advised to follow if they hope to achieve any credibility that stands up to serious investigation. It appears that Eysenck and Nias, unlike Kurtz and his colleagues, had no preconceptions they were attempting to defend. Theirs was truly what could be called a *scientific* investigation in the best sense of the word.

On November 17, 1995, I sent a copy of the above portion of my appendix to Professor Kurtz for his comments and, in an attempt at fairness, to give him an opportunity to defend himself against my accusations. What I received in reply from one of his assistants was an almost book-length defense—regarding a completely different article! The book I referred to here was totally ignored in their reply. The article they defended against, "sTARBABY: The Great Debunking Scandal," appeared in *Fate Magazine*, October, 1981. It was written by Dennis Rawlins, a former colleague of Prof Kurtz and his CSICOP. It begins with, "They call themselves the Committee for the Scientific Investigation of Claims of the Paranormal. In fact, they are a group of would-be debunkers who bungled their major investigation, falsified the results, covered up their errors, and gave the boot to a colleague who threatened to tell the truth."

APPENDIX II

THE REAPPEARANCE OF THE WHAT???[2]

THE RECENT APPEARANCE of a full-page advertisement in the *New York Times*, as well as in several other large circulation newspapers around the world, proclaims the imminent reappearance of the Christ in a physical, human body.

How tempting it is to embrace the promises of Benjamin Crème who, in his book *The Reappearance of the Christ and the Masters of Wisdom*, states that Christ himself will appear publicly on radio and television and end the problems of inflation, unemployment, political unrest and world hunger that pervade our planet at this time.

> One day soon, men and women all over the world will gather round their radio and television sets to hear and see the Christ: to see His face, and to hear His words dropping silently into their minds—in their own language. . . . His task, and that of His Disciples, the Masters of the Wisdom, will be to inaugurate the age of Reason, the age of Brotherhood, the age of Love, and so bring men into full conscious awareness of themselves as integral parts of the One Divine Life.[3]

The promises held forth sound almost too good to be true: "And in response to His message, millions throughout the world will form themselves into groups for the active promotion of goodwill. From being, at present, a minority, they will grow into an overwhelming majority, demanding an end to separation, hatred, and injustice. The potency of hatred, mounting now to a climax, will be opposed by this active movement of Goodwill. The groups in the Five Centers, stimulated by the Master resident in each, will spread the radiance of the Christ's Message: Sharing, Justice, Cooperation, Goodwill—the keynotes of the New Age" (P 66). Not only that, but in conjunction with this event, the "emergence of the Hierarchy" will also take place, a process that takes about thirty years to accomplish. Included in this group are some sixty-three Masters, between four and five hundred Adepts of the fourth Initiation, between two and three thousand Initiates of the third, around 250,000 of the second, and about 800,000 who have taken the first Initiation. These enlightened beings will help show us how to achieve this state of paradise on Earth, not only in the fields of religion and the arts, but also in politics, science, and education.

Since March 1974, Mr. Crème has been delivering this message of hope to ever-widening circles. Today we find him traveling all over the world and, with the aid of radio, television, and newspaper advertising, reaching hundreds of thousands, if not millions of would-be believers.

It's probably a safe assumption to say that all normal, healthy, clear-thinking people want peace on Earth, as well as the age of Reason, the age of Brotherhood, and all the other good things Mr. Crème says are in store for us. It's probably even safer to say that the needy, the hungry, and the oppressed want these things even more than those not oppressed. But is simply wanting something enough? Is it enough to simply read or hear about these great promises and then wait for them to happen? What are we really doing by accepting this promised paradise?

We will consider two important questions raised in the book itself: the first concerns the divinity of Christ, and the second deals with the actual nature of the Second Coming.

"The Christ is not the name of an individual but of an Office in the Hierarchy" says Mr. Crème "The present holder of that office, the Lord Maitreya, has held it for 2,600 years, and manifested in Palestine through His Disciple, Jesus, by the occult method of overshadowing" (p. 30). He further states, "The Christ took over the body of Jesus and manifested through it for the last three years. The Christ, Maitreya, remained in the Himalayas, but His consciousness, or some aspect of His consciousness, whatever was needed at the time, took over the body of the disciple Jesus and worked through Him for the last three years of His life. This time He has come Himself" (p. 53).

Now, what Mr. Crème is saying (if I read him correctly) is that there was no crucifixion of Christ two thousand years ago. That Christ (or "Christ-Maitreya," as Crème calls him) was actually thousands of miles away in a Himalayan retreat while Jesus, the man, was being crucified at Golgotha. In fact he goes further, stating explicitly that Christ is not God. "The Christ is not God. When I say 'the coming of Christ,' I don't mean the coming of God; I mean the coming of a divine man, a man who has manifested His divinity by the same process that we are going through—the incarnational process, gradually perfecting Himself; the Initiatory process, gradually becoming more and more divine" (p. 115). And again: "Christ is not God. He is not coming as God [and] I think He would rather you didn't pray to Him" (P. 135). And finally, he calls him a guru (p. 118) and a simple man (p. 12). So now we know what we're accepting (or rather, what we're not accepting) when we believe in Mr. Crème's "Christ"; in essence, we are rejecting the divinity of Christ.

Furthermore, for two millennia now, the faithful have been taking Holy Communion, believing, as the real Christ said, "This is my body ... this is my blood." Now, if we believe Mr. Crème, we learn that it was not Christ's body or his blood, and that Christ was thousands of miles away during that crucial moment in Earth's history when Jesus was crucified, buried, and resurrected. For this is what Mr. Crème is saying when you really think about it: that not only was there no crucifixion of Christ, but there was no resurrection of Christ either. In other words, by embracing Mr. Crème's message and believing it, we are simply declaring two thousand years of Christian tradition a hoax.

It is not the purpose of this short review to place any blame on Mr. Crème (who, by the way, as these lines are being typed, is just a few blocks away in preparation for a television interview here in Buffalo tomorrow morning.) Nor would it in any way be productive to make this an emotional issue. Mr. Crème may well be an unwitting tool of other individuals who are using his telepathic faculties to their advantage.

The reader may recall the rather sudden rise to infamy of a young Eastern guru who, during the mid-seventies, declared himself "The Divine Lord of the Universe." His popularity waxed considerably until he was caught smuggling jewels into India. Shortly thereafter his mother, whom he had proclaimed "The Divine Mother," disowned him because of his errant ways. This brings us to the second question; What is the true nature of the Second Coming? Again, this is an emotional and highly speculative issue for some people, so we will attempt to deal with it as rationally and factually as possible.

This question must be dealt with because of Mr. Crème's statement that "total belief that all of this is true is not essential. An open-minded acceptance of the *possibility* of the Christ's return now is the overriding necessity at the present time" (p. 38). Well, obviously we cannot ignore such a strong, pivotal statement of Mr. Crème's thesis. All we have to do is believe that it can happen, and it will. This is a deceptively simple position for him to take, however, and one that requires a bit of investigation before we can shed light on why our mere acceptance of the possibility of such an event is all that is needed for it to actually take place.

Many of us might be tempted to simply admit to the possibility and then dismiss the matter from any further thought. This is precisely what Mr. Crème's leaders would like us to do: accept the possibility of Christ's return in a physical body, even though the Bible says he will appear in the clouds. But Mr. Crème goes a bit too far when we read, "He came into the world by aeroplane and so fulfilled the prophecy of 'coming in the clouds.' On July 8th 1977, He descended from the Himalaya(s) into the Indian sub-continent and went to one of the chief cities there" (p. 55). Is that all that "coming in the clouds" means? Anybody with a few hundred rupees can do that. No, there is a much greater significance to this question.

It is interesting that the short passage just quoted comes immediately after a member of his audience asked him a question about Rudolf Steiner. The question was: "Rudolf Steiner seems to say that the Christ would not come in a physical body. Were there changes made after that?" (P 54). Mr. Crème's answer: "Yes. Rudolf Steiner died in 1925. The announcement of the Christ's desire to return to the world was made in 1945. The decision to reappear was made earlier, but the mode of the reappearance was not determined." He goes on to say that four disciples were being prepared—gradually overshadowed—to be possible vehicles for the Christ, but that this plan was later abandoned. Crème is implying that, at the last minute (cosmically speaking) before the second most momentous event in human history, Christ changed his mind and decided to reappear in a different way. He then decided to manifest his own physical body and take an airplane.

In one short paragraph, not only are Rudolf Steiner's arguments dismissed, but he, Steiner, is also accused (by inference) of having been totally misguided on the question of Christ and of his reappearance.

Readers who are familiar with the life and work of Rudolf Steiner know that he cannot be dismissed in such a summary fashion. During the first quarter of the twentieth century, Steiner patiently and with meticulous care formulated the groundwork for a very precise science of the spirit. The central core of his system of thought was the unique, divine nature of Christ and the central, pivotal event in human evolution that occurred two thousand years ago when, as God, he walked the Earth in a physical body. Readers who have the patience and open mind to work their way through perhaps twenty or thirty of his books begin to grasp the fact that Steiner was not just speculating. He spoke and wrote from direct spiritual vision. Several times in his writings, Steiner warns of the coming of a false messiah who, toward the end of the twentieth century, would declare that he is the Christ, appearing in a physical body. The acceptance of this being as the Christ, he says, will be attributable to a completely materialistic worldview.

Humanity is evolving, and what was appropriate two thousand years ago is no longer possible now. Christ will reappear, but his appearance will be to increasingly higher planes of perception, not on the physical level. During the next three thousand years, Christ will be apprehended increasingly by the more highly developed souls on Earth.

In conclusion, then, we must realize that in Crème and his co-workers we are not dealing with a small, insignificant band of amateur occultists. The declaration of Christ's physical return to Earth is part of a well-organized plan many years in the making. The positive aspect of this is that, in confronting such a powerful temptation (the acceptance of Crème's promises of bliss and the end of worldly problems), we are called on to become conscious of the real events behind the scenes. By facing such promises of paradise without succumbing to their temptations, we take a step forward in our evolution as human beings. The divinity of Christ remains a fact, whether we accept it or not. The healthy course of human evolution is to strive continually for an ever-increasing perception of life's realities and to hold fast to our course, whatever our temptations may be.

What can you do? For one, the following bibliography lists a number of fundamental works and helpful lectures by Rudolf Steiner. A close, unbiased, and serious study of these and other anthroposophic works can begin the process of opening the reader's mind to greater possibilities and, more important, guide the reader along a path of inner development that is sure and safe. (See the Bibliography following the endnotes.)

Notes

SEE BIBLIOGRAPHY FOR PUBLICATION INFORMATION

Preface

1. Pascal, Blaise, *Pens es*.

Chapter 1 – The Two Faces of Evil

1. Troward's original phrase: "These things are not true because they are written in the Bible, but the Bible is true because these things are written in it." *The Law and the Word*, p. 181.
2. Aurobindo, *The Hour of God and Other Writings*, p. 91.
3. *Paradise Lost*, Book IV, lines 246–260.
4. Steiner, "The Concepts of Original Sin and Grace."
5. Aurobindo, *Letters on Yoga*, vol I, p. 381.
6. Steiner, *Three Streams in the Evolution of Mankind. The Connection of the Luciferic-Ahrimanic Impulses with the Christ-Jahve Impulse*.
7. Aurobindo, *Op. cit. The Hour of God* ... p. 85.
8. Steiner, *Op. cit. Three Streams* ...
9. *Ibid.*, pp.19, 20.
10. Cooke, Maurice B., (from Hilarion), *Dark Robes, Dark Brothers*, p. 1.

Chapter 2 – A Closer Look

1. A growing number of authors and social commentators are now warning us of the dangers of television and computers, particularly in the hands of our children. Here are a few worthy of note: Jerry Mander, *Four Arguments for the Elimination of Television*, and the curiously titled *In the Absence of the Sacred: The Failure of Technology and the Survival of the Indian Nations*. See also Stephen Talbott's *The Future Does Not Compute: Transcending the Machines in our Midst*. From a spiritual scientific perspective, see the difficult but occasionally brilliant monograph, "The Computer and the Incarnation of Ahriman" by David B. Black (see bibliography).
2. Steiner, *The Influence of Lucifer and Ahriman: Man's Responsibility for the Earth*, p. 11.
3. All great spiritual teachers have followed this path of self-sacrifice rather than of self-love or self-service. Paramahansa Yogananda, for example, lays bare his soul in his poem "God's Boatman," where he makes a similar prom-

ise: / ... Oh, I will come again and again! / Crossing a million crags of suffering. / With bleeding feet, I will come— / If need be, a trillion times— / So long as I know / One stray brother is left behind...." (Published in *Self Realization Fellowship*, Yogoda Satsanga Sociaty of India, Golden Anniversary, Self-Realization Fellowship, Los Angeles, 1970, p. 75). Another notable example is St. Therese of Lisieux who, shortly before her death exclaimed to Mother Agnes, "I will return! I will come down! ... I feel that my mission is about to begin, my mission of making others love God as I love Him, my mission of teaching my little ways to souls. If God answers my requests, my heaven will be spent on Earth up until the end of the world. Yes, I want to spend my heaven in doing good on Earth." *(Story of a Soul: The Autobiography of St. Therese of Lisieux,* translated from the original by John Clark, O.C.D., ICS (Institute of Carmelite Studies) Publications, Washington, DC, 1975, p. 263).

4. Steiner, *Op. cit.*
5. Lectures 9 & 10, *Karmic Relationship.* vol. 3.
6. *Ibid.* lecture 9, p. 146.
7. *Ibid.* lecture 10, pp. 158–9.
8. *Ibid,* lectures 7 & 8.
9, See for example, R. Steiner, *The Archangel Michael: His Mission and Ours.*
10. Steiner, *The Wrong and Right Use of Esoteric Knowledge,* lecture 1.
11. Heidenreich, Alfred, *The Book of Revelation,* p. 123.
12. *Karmic Relationships,* vol 6, pp. 176–7.

CHAPTER 3 – A HOLOSCOPIC LOOK AT THE HUMAN BEING

1. Random House, New York, 1999.
2. Diet, too—especially when laden with chemical food additives, pesticides and fertilizers—is said to contribute to such behavior. See for instance *The Crazy Makers: How the Food Industry is Destroying Our Brains and Harming Our Children,* by Carol Simontacchi, Tharcher, New York, 2000.
3. Penguin Putnam, New York, 1977.
4. This work is presently translated as a volume titled *Intuitive Thinking as a Spiritual Path: A Philosophy of Freedom.* A previous edition was also translated into English, at his suggestion, as *The Philosophy of Spiritual Activity.*
5. *Occult Science and Occult Development,* pp. 13–14.
6. *The Karma of Materialism,* pp. 144–5.
7. Aurobindo, *The Future Evolution of Man: The Divine Life upon Earth,* pp. 85–6.
8. *The Analects of Confucius,* XIV:30 (28 in some translations).
9. See, for example, "Requirements for Esoteric Training," *How to Know Higher Worlds: A Modern Path of Initiation.*
10. "The Six Protective Exercises with their Etheric Powers," *Newsletter,* Anthroposophical Society in America, winter, 1986–7.
11. Woodstock, NY, Overlook Press, 1999, p. 42.

12. New York, Penguin Putnam, 2001.
13. New York, St. Martin's, 2002.
14. Lindsey Tanner, *Associated Press* release, June 5, 2002.
15. Goethe, Johann Wolfgang von, *The Metamorphosis of Plants*, Junction City, OR, Biodynamic Farming and Gardening Assoc., 1993. Further elaboration of this work was accomplished by Gerbert Grohmann in his *The Plant: A Guide to Understanding its Nature*, Wyoming RI, Biodynamic Literature, 1996.
16. See Steiner, "The Lord's Prayer, Considered Esoterically," *The Christian Mysteries: Early Lectures*, 1998. See also his "The Structure of the Lord's Prayer."
17. *Op. cit., Influence of Spiritual Beings.*
18. *Ibid.*
19. Steiner, *Nature Spirits*, pp. 75–6.

Chapter 4 – The Eternal Feminine

1. Christy Barnes, *The Threefold Review*, no. 13, p. 29. See also James J, Kilpatrick's "The Great Dilemma: Gender and Pronouns," in his syndicated "Writer's Art" column, July 7, 1997, in which he suggests that when all else fails we "plunge into the vortex" and use the masculine-sounding pronoun.
2. Steiner, *Happenings at the Turn of the Milennia.*
3. For a first-hand account of these times, see: "The Man, Rudolf Steiner" by Andrei Balyi, in the *Journal for Anthroposophy*, no 28, autumn, 1978.
4. As quoted by Arthur Zajonc in "Kingdoms of Earth, Chorus of Christ," *Newsletter*, Anthroposophical Society in America, winter, 1994–5, p. 4.
5. Steiner, *The Search for the New Isis: The Divine Sophia.*
6. A moment's reflection shows us that the Three Kings were initiates. For how could a *physical* star have led them to a tiny cave or stable without causing a great deal of public alarm? That would have left many external, historical references, to say the least. It is obvious that this was an inner, a spiritual, star that only they could see. For more on this subject, see the Christmas lectures in Steiner's *Festivals and their Meaning.*
7. *The Being of Man and His Future Evolution*, lecture II, "Illness and Karma"
8. *Op. cit., Nature Spirits*, pp. 75–6.

Chapter 5 – Repentance, the Ultimate Paradigm Shift

1. In Henley's words, from his "Invictus": "Beyond this place of wrath and tears / Looms but the horror of the shade. / And yet the menace of the years / Finds, and shall find me, unafraid. / It matters not how strait the gate, / How charged with punishments the scroll, / I am the master of my fate: / I am the captain of my soul."
2. Aurobindo, *Op. cit., The Hour of God*, chapter 4, "Thoughts and Aphorisms, p. 82.

3. Aurobindo, *Op. cit., Letters on Yoga*, p. 162
4. New Century Bank, 513 Kimberton Rd., Phoenixville, PA 19460, www.newcenturybank.com. Careful here, there are several "New Century Banks."
5. Schumacher, *Small is Beautiful*, p. 85.
6. Steiner, *Op.cit., Influence of Spiritual Beings*, pp. 44–46.
7. A valuable resource in this regard is Steiner's lecture course *The Gospel of St. John* (see bibliography).
8. *Harpers Magazine*, Oct 1997.
9. Avogadro's Law states that the number of molecules in a gram-molecule of any substance equals 6.054×10^{23}. The first dilution of one one-hundredth will reduce this to 6.054×10^{21}. After the twelfth dilution, therefore (twenty-fourth dilution if decimal, or one in ten, fractions are taken), according to this law there will be no molecules left of the original substance. Yet the effects of the medication persist. A number of excellent books offer a much fuller treatment of this subject: see, for example, Dr. Michael Weiner, *The Complete Book of Homeopathy*, Avery Publishing, New York, 1989.
10. Benveniste, Jacques: *Comptes Rendus de l'Academie des Sciences*, Paris, 312, II (1991) pp. 461–466. E. Devenas et al., "Human Basophil Degranulation Triggered by Very Dilute Antiserum Against Age." *Nature*, 334 (July 28, 1988), pp. 287–290.
11. See, for example, "French Scientist Reports Research," in *Homeopathic Research Reports*, winter, 1991/1992.
12. "Is Homeopathy Science?" *Homeopathy Today*, April, 1993.
13. *American Scientist*, vol. 81 (March/April 1993).
14. As quoted by Ernst Lehrs in his highly recommended *Man or Matter*.

Chapter 6 – Restitution and Redemption

1. The Christian Community Church, or "Movement for Religious Renewal," was begun in Europe under the guidance of Rudolf Steiner. It was intended to be a religious devotional path for modern times. See James H. Hindes, *Renewing Christianity*, Steinerbooks, 1995.
2. *Harper's Bible Dictionary*, Harper & Row, 1985, p. 502.
3. *Smith's Bible Dictionary*, Holt, Reinhart and Winston, New York, Chicago & San Francisco, 1948.
4. *Oxford Study Edition: The New English Bible with the Apocrypha*, New York: Oxford University Press, 1976.
5. *The Dartmouth Bible*, 2nd ed., Boston: Houghton Miflin, 1961.
6. McCausland, Bruce H. "The Reappearance of the What???" *Inner Life*, Toronto's Aquarian Age Newsletter, vol. 8, no. 9 (June, 1982). [See appendix II].

Chapter 7 — The After-Image

1. A good example of this is found in John E. Dale, "Power Plants: Sorting out the Frenzied Cellular Process That Leads to the Growth of Leaves," *The Sciences*, New York Academy of Sciences, September/October, 1994, p. 28. To be sure, some writers in popular magazines still consider Goethe a bit mad as a scientist; see, for example, Sue Hubbell, "How Taxonomy Helps Us Make Sense out of the Natural World," *The Smithsonian*, May, 1996, (vol. 27, no. 2).
2. For a fuller and more comprehensive introduction to these matters the reader is referred to several works. Perhaps the simplest are Rudolf Steiner's *Founding a Science of the Spirit* and *Rosicrucian Wisdom: An Introduction*. For a much more definitive treatment see his *Outline of Esoteric Science*, chapter 4.
3. Steiner, *The Festivals and their Meaning*, "Christmas." In lecture 7 we find: "Behold the Sun / At the midnight hour; / Build with stones the lifeless ground. / Thus in decay and in the night of Death / Find the Creation's strength; / Glory in the heights the eternal Word of Gods; / Shelter in depths the Powers of Peace. / In Darkness dwelling, create a Sun. / In matter weaving, know the joy of Spirit!" See also Edouard Schur's description of initiation in the "Eleusinian Mysteries" in the section on Plato in his book *The Great Initiates: A Study of the Secret History of Religions*.
4. Jacques Lusseyran, *And There Was Light: The Autobiography of a Blind Hero in the French Resistance*, Morning Light Press, Sandpoint, ID, 1998.
5. Steiner, *The Apocalypse of St. John*.
6. Steiner, *The Book of Revelation: And the Work of the Priest*, 18 lectures to priests, Dornach, September 5–22, 1924 (CW 346).
7. Miceli, Vincent P. S. J., *The Antichrist*.

Chapter 8 — Mysterium Magnum

1. See also Dawkins' "God's Utility Function," *Scientific American*, Nov. 1995.

Chapter 9 — Thoughtworthy Themes

1. Joseph Fletcher, *Situation Ethics: The New Morality*, Westminster Press, 1966.
2. See Joseph Fletcher, *William Temple: Twentieth-Century Christian*, Seabury Press, 1963, pp. 80–82, 316–318.
3. Steiner, *The Being of Man and his Future Evolution*.
4. Margenau, Henry, and Roy Abraham Varghese, eds., *Cosmos, Bios, Theos: Scientists Reflect on Science, God, and the Origins of the Universe, Life, and Homo Sapiens*, Open Court, Chicago, 1992.
5. See especially, Rudolf Steiner, *Secret Brotherhoods: And the Mystery of the Human Double*.
6. *Ibid.*

Appendices

1. Eysenck, H. J., and D. K. Nias, *Astrology: Science or Superstition?* St Martin's Press, New York, 1982, p. 202.
2. The June, 1982 issue of *Inner Life, Toronto's Aquarian Age Newsletter* (vol. 8, no. 9) is not likely to be available for your perusal. The lead article therefore, written by this author, is reproduced here as appendix II in a slightly edited form.
3. Crème, Benjamin, *The Reappearance of the Christ and the Masters of Wisdom*, Tara Center, Los Angeles, 1980, p. 37.

Bibliography

Note: SB = SteinerBooks (Anthroposophic Press), Great Barrington, MA; RSP = Rudolf Steiner Press, London; SBC = Steiner Book Centre, North Vancouver. CW = Collected Works (GA, or *Gasamptausbgabe*, in the original German collection). All works, if in print, are available from SteinerBooks (www.steinerbooks.org).

Achtemeier, Paul, *Harper's Bible Dictionary*, HarperCollins, New York, 1985.
Adams, George, *Physical and Ethereal Spaces*, RSP, 1965.
Asten, H. Keller von, *Encounter with the Infinite: Geometrical Experiences through Active Contemplation*, Walter Keller, Dornach, Switzerland, 1973.
Aurobindo, Sri, *The Future Evolution of Man: The Divine Life upon Earth*, Quest, Wheaton, 1963.
———, *The Hour of God and Other Writings*, vol. 17, Sri Aurobindo Birth Centenary Library - Popular Edition, Sri Aurobindo Ashram, Pondicherry, 1972.
———, *Letters on Yoga*, part one, Sri Aurobindo Ashram, Pondicherry, India, 1971.
Barnes, Christy, "To Be or Not to Be Human," *The Threefold Review*, no 13, p, 29.
Basham, Don, *Deliver Us From Evil: A Pastor's Reluctant Encounters With The Powers Of Darkness*, Chosen Books, Wheaton, IL, 2005.
Belyi, Andrei, "The Man, Rudolf Steiner," *Journal for Anthroposophy*, No 28, Autumn, 1978.
Benveniste, Jacques, "Comptes Rendus de l'Academie des Sciences," Paris, 312, II (1991) 461-466.
Blatty, Peter, *The Exorcist*, Bantam Books, New York, 1971.
Bock, Emil, *The Apocalypse of Saint John*, Floris Books, Edinburgh, 2006.
Bronowski, Diederich, et al, "Is Homeopathy Science?" *Homeopathy Today*, April 1993 (cited by Julian Winston).
Brown, Courtney, *Cosmic Explorers: Scientific Remote Viewing, Extraterrestrials, and a Message for Mankind*, Dutton, 1999.
Bugliarello, George, "Five Hundred Years Later," *American Scientist*, vol. 81 (March/April, 1993), lead editorial.
Chamberlin, Roy B., *Dartmouth Bible*, 2nd ed., Houghton Mifflin, Boston, 2000.
Clarke, Arthur C., *Childhood's End*, Harcourt Brace, New York, 1953.
Confucius, *Analects* (My own rendering from various translations).
Dawkins, Richard, *The Blind Watchmaker*, Oxford University Press, Oxford, UK, 1986.

———, *Climbing Mount Improbable*, Oxford University Press, Oxford, UK, 1996.
———, *The Selfish Gene*, Oxford University Press, Oxford, UK, 1976.
Devenas, E., et al., "Human Basophil Degranulation Triggered by Very Dilute Antiserum against Age." *Nature*, 334 (July 28, 1988) 287–290. Also see "French Scientist Reports Research" in *Homeopathic Research Reports*, winter, 1991–1992.
Drew, Elizabeth, *The Corruption of American Politics: What Went Wrong and Why*, Overlook Press, New York, 2000.
Ehrenfeld, David, "A Techno-Pox upon the Land," *Harper's Magazine*, Oct., 1997.
Eysenck, Hans J., and D. K. Nias. *Astrology: Science or Superstition?* St. Martin's Press, New York, 1982.
Fernández-Armesto, Felipe, *Truth: A History and a Guide for the Perplexed*, St. Martin's Press, NY, 1999.
Fletcher, Joseph F., *Situation Ethics: The New Morality*. Westminster Press, Philadelphia, 1966.
———, *William Temple: Twentieth-Century Christian*, Alec R. Allenson, Westville, FL, 1963.
Garrett, Laurie, *The Coming Plague: Newly Emerging Diseases in a World Out of Balance*, Penguin Books, New York, 1995.
Glasser, William, MD., *Reality Therapy: A New Approach to Psychiatry*. Harper & Row, New York, 1965.
Goethe, *Faust*, Walter Kaufmann translator and introduction, Doubleday Anchor, New York, 1963.
Grosssman, Lt. Col. Dave, and Gloria DeGaetano, *Stop Teaching Our Kids to Kill: A Call to Action against TV, Movie & Video Game Violence*, Crown, New York, 1999.
Heidenreich, Alfred, *The Book of Revelation*, Floris Books, Edinburgh, 1977.
Hilarion (Maurice B. Cooke), *Dark Robes, Dark Brothers*, Marcus Books, Toronto, 1981.
Hindes, James H., *Renewing Christianity*, SB, 1995.
Holdrege, Craig, *Genetics and the Manipulation of Life: The Forgotten Factor of Context*, Lindisfarne Books, Great Barrington, MA, 1996.
Kurtz, Paul, in *Objections to Astrology*. Prometheus, Buffalo, 1975.
Lehrs, Ernst, *Man or Matter: Introduction to a Spiritual Understanding of Nature on the Basis of Goethe's "Method of Training Observation and Thought,"* 3rd ed., RSP, London, 1958.
Lewin, Roger, *Complexity: Life at the Edge of Chaos*, Macmillan, New York, 1992.
Lowell, James Russell, "The Present Crisis," *The Poems of James Russell Lowell*, Kessinger, Whitefish, MT, 2004.
Lozano, Neal, *Unbound: a Practical Guide to Deliverance from Evil Spirits*, Chosen Books, Wheaton, IL, 2003.
Luna, Felix, *Navidad Nuestra (Our Christmas) Oratorio*, (words from church bulletin), translator unknown.
Lusseyran, Jacques, *And There Was Light: Autobiography of Jacques Lusseyran, Blind Hero of the French Resistance*, Morning Light Press, Sandpoint, ID, 1998.
Margenau, Henry, and Roy Abraham Varghese, eds., *Cosmos, Bios, Theos: Scientists Reflect on Science, God, and the Origins of the Universe, Life, and Homo Sapiens*, Open Court Press, Peru, IL, 1992.

McCausland, Bruce, "Reappearance of the What???" *Inner Life Magazine*, Toronto's Aquarian Age Newsletter, vol. 8, no. 9, June, 1982 (see appendix 2).
Miceli, Vincent P., S. J., *The Antichrist*, Roman Catholic Books, Harrison, NY 1981.
Millman, Dan, and Doug Childers, *Divine Interventions: True Stories of Mystery and Miracles That Change Lives*, Daybreak Books, Emmaus, 1999.
Milton, John, *Paradise Lost*, John Leonard, trans., Penguin Classics, New York, 2003.
Mundy, Alicia, *Dispensing with the Truth: The Victims, the Drug Companies, and the Dramatic Story Behind the Battle over Fen-Phen*, St. Martin's, New York, 2001.
Oxford University, *New English Bible with the Apocrypha, The*, Oxford Study Edition, Oxford University Press, New York, 1976.
Pascal, Blaise, *Pensées*, Dutton, New York, 1958.
Peck, M. Scott, *People of the Lie: The Hope for Healing Human Evil*, Touchstone, New York, 1985.
Raloff, Janet, "When Science and Beliefs Collide" *Science News*, vol. 149.
Rampton, Sheldon, and John Stauber, *Trust Us, We're Experts! How Industry Manipulates Science and Gambles with Your Future*, Tarcher, New York, 2001.
Rawlins, Dennis, "TARBABY," *Fate Magazine*, October 1981, pp 67–98.
Ridley, Matt, *The Origins of Virtue: Human Instincts and the Evolution of Cooperation*, Penguin, New York, 1997.
Rifkin, Jeremy, *The Biotech Century: Harnessing the Gene and Remaking the World*, Tarcher, New York, 1999.
Rue, Loyal, *By the Grace of Guile: The Role of Deception in Natural History and Human Affairs*, Oxford University Press, New York, 1994.
Ruskin, John, "The Storm-Cloud of the Nineteenth Century," as quoted by Ernst Lehrs in *Man or Matter*.
Schumacher, E. F., *Good Work*, Harper, New York 1979.
———, *Small Is Beautiful: Economics as if People Mattered*, HarperCollins, New York, 1975.
Schuré, Edouard, *The Great Initiates: A Study of the Secret History of Religions*, Garber Books, Blauvelt, NY, 1976.
Simontacchi, Carol, *The Crazy Makers: How the Food Industry Is Destroying Our Brains and Harming our Children*, Tarcher, New York, 2000.
Smith, William, *Smith's Bible Dictionary*, Nelson Reference, Nashville, TN, 2004.
Sparrow, G. Scott, *I Am With You Always*, Bantam Books, New York, 1995.
Steiner, Rudolf (See below).
Sun-Tzu, *The Art of War*, Shambhala, Boston, 2001.
Tanner, Lindsey, "Leading Medical Journal Launches Criticism of Published Studies", Associated Press syndicated article, June 5, 2002.
Threefold Review, published by the Margaret Fuller Corporation, PO Box 6, Philmont, NY, 12565.
Tipler, Frank, J. *Physics of Immortality: Modern Cosmology, God, and the Resurrection of the Dead*. Doubleday, New York, 1994.
Troward, Judge Thomas, *The Law and the Word*, Dodd, Mead, New York, 1917.
Watson, Lyall, *Dark Nature: A Natural History of Evil*, Harper, New York, 1995.
Wicher, Olive, *Creative Polarities in Space and Time*, RSP, London, 1971.
Wilson, John, *Language and the Pursuit of Truth*, Cambridge University Press, New York, 1969.
Winn, Marie, *The Plug-in Drug: Television, Children, & the Family*, Penguin, New York, 2002.

Zajonc, Arthur, *Catching the Light: The Entwined History of Light and Mind*. Oxford University Press, New York, 1993.

Books by Rudolf Steiner

The Archangel Michael: His Mission and Ours, selected lectures and writings, SB, 1994.
The Being of Man and His Future Evolution, 9 lectures, Berlin 1908–1909 (CW 107), RSP, 1981.
The Book of Revelation: And the Work of the Priest, 18 lectures to priests, Dornach, September 5–22, 1924 (CW 346), RSP, 1998.
The Festivals and their Meaning, a collection of lectures, RSP, 2002.
Foundations of Esotericism, 31 lectures, Berlin, September 26–November 5, 1905 (CW 93a) RSP, 1983.
Founding a Science of the Spirit, 14 lectures, Stuttgart, Aug. 22–Sept. 4, 1906 (CW 95), RSP, 1999. Previous edition, *At the Gates of Spiritual Science*.
"Concepts of Original Sin and Grace," 1 lecture, May 3, 1911, Anthroposophical Publishing Company, London, 1960.
The Gospel of St. John, 12 lectures, Hamburg, May 5–31, 1908 (CW 103), SB 1962.
Happenings at the Turn of the Millennium, MS S-2899 (152) Ref: London Z-344; available from Rudolf Steiner Library, Ghent, NY.
How to Know Higher Worlds: A Modern Path of Initiation, written 1904-1905 (CW 10), SB, 1994; previous edition *Knowledge of the Higher Worlds and its Attainment*.
Influence of Spiritual Beings upon Man, The, 11 lectures, Berlin, January 6–June 11, 1908 (CW 102), SB, 1961.
The Influences of Lucifer and Ahriman: Human Responsibility for the Earth, 5 lectures, 1919 (CWs 191 & 193), SB, 1993.
Intuitive Thinking as a Spiritual Path: A Philosophy of Freedom, SB, written 1894 (CW 4) 1995; previous edition *The Philosophy of Spiritual Activity*.
The Karma of Materialism, 9 lectures, Berlin, July 31–Sept. 25, 1917 (CW 176), SB, 1985.
Karmic Relationships, Esoteric Studies, vols. 3 (11 lectures, Dornach, July 1–August 8, 1924, CW 237), 4 (11 lectures, Dornach, September 5–24 1924, CW 238), 5, (7 lectures, Prague & Paris, March 29–May 25, 1924, CW 239), RSP, 1997, 2002.
Nature Spirits: Selected Lectures, RSP, 2003.
"Occult Science and Occult Development"; "Christ at the Time of the Mystery of Golgotha & Christ in the Twentieth Century," 2 lectures, London, May 1 & 2, 1913 (CW 233), RSP 1966.
An Outline of Esoteric Science, written 1910 (CW 13), SB, 1997; previous edition *Occult Science: An Outline*.
Prayer, SB, 1966.
Rosicrucian Wisdom: An Introduction, 14 lectures, Munich, May 22–June 6, 1907 (CW 99). RSP, 2000; a previous edition was titled *Theosophy of the Rosicrucian*.
"The Search for the New Isis: The Divine Sophia," in *The Goddess: From Natura to the Divine Sophia*, selected lectures, RSP, 2002.

Secret Brotherhoods: And the Mystery of the Human Double, 7 lectures, St. Gallen, Zurich, and Dornach, November 15–25, 1917 (CW 178), RSP, 2004.
Secrets of the Threshold, 8 lectures, August 24–31, 1913 (CW 147), SB, 1987.
The Spiritual Hierarchies and the Physical World: Zodiac, Planets & Cosmos, 10 lectures, 1909 (CW 110), SB 2007.
Three Streams in the Evolution of Mankind: The Connection of the Luciferic-Ahrimanic Impulses with the Christ-Jahve Impulse, lecture, Dornach, Oct. 4-13, 1918 (CW 184), RSP, 1965.
The Wrong and Right Use of Esoteric Knowledge, 3 lectures, Dornach, November 18–25, 1917 (CW 178), RSP, 1966.

FOR FURTHER STUDY ON THE SUBJECT OF THE DOUBLE (DOPPELGÄNGER) (REFERRED TO IN CHAPTER NINE) ALL WORKS BY RUDOLF STEINER:

Foundations of Esotericism, lecture 2.
Founding a Science of the Spirit, lecture three; this wide-ranging cycle of lectures provides a good introduction to Anthroposophy in general.
Secrets of the Threshold, lecture 7.
The Spiritual Hierarchies; for a discussion of elemental beings generally, see lecture 2.
The Wrong and Right Use of Esoteric Knowledge.

www.ingramcontent.com/pod-product-compliance
Lightning Source LLC
Chambersburg PA
CBHW031145160426
43193CB00008B/255